Praise for *A Holistic Guide to Onli...*

"It's pretty tough today to create a comprehensive look at online marketing. The complexities, channels and quickly shifting best practices make it a tall order. But Joey Donovan Guido has done it! The book is filled with relevant examples and recommendations for improving this vital aspect of your marketing."
— *Drew McLellan, Co-founder of McLellan Marketing Group*

"The book is truly relevant for both newcomers to the marketing profession, as well as seasoned professionals, as it accurately covers a wide breadth of online marketing methodologies. In addition, there are many real-world examples to back Joey's solid strategies, which makes learning about SEO, user experience and conversion easier and more enjoyable. I highly recommend this book!"
— *Wayne Breitbarth, author of the best-selling book* The Power Formula for LinkedIn Success

"This is a must-read crash course for online marketing, especially if you are new to marketing. Author Joey Donovan Guido keeps your attention with illustrative stories and entertaining metaphors, while backing up his advice about SEO, user experience and conversion with concrete research. Even digitally-savvy practitioners like myself will find themselves making a list of critical things to improve upon."
— *Drew Neisser, Founder & CEO of Renegade LLC, author, host of* Renegade Thinkers Unite *podcast*

"As someone who lives and breathes this stuff, I can honestly say that Joey Donovan Guido's book, which covers SEO, is not only one of the most comprehensive on this subject, but one of the easiest to understand with tons of actionable insights. Most importantly, he understands that SEO is not just a technical subject, but a human one, and that it all starts with your customer. Sure, there is lots of technical stuff covered, but he ties it in with how it affects the people who visit your site. If you are a business owner looking to improve your search rankings, or you are a web designer wondering how to get better results for your clients, read this book and keep it for a reference."

— *Greg Jameson, President of WebStores Ltd, best-selling author, Colorado Small Business of the Year*

"When Joey says 'holistic,' he isn't kidding. This book should be required reading for business owners and marketing folks just starting out. Joey lays out a complete and actionable step-by-step guide to SEO, UX, and conversion for your website, blog and social media channels. If you feel lost when it comes to SEO, UX, and/or conversion, this is the place to start!"

— *Jon-Mikel Bailey, President of Wood Street Web Design & Development*

"Beginner and veteran marketers will pick up important tips on SEO, user experience and conversion in this comprehensive book. I appreciate Joey's conversational tone and his anecdotes to explain high-level marketing concepts. It's clear he has brought success to his clients with the strategies he outlines."

— *Brian Lee, APR, President of Revelation PR, Advertising & Social Media*

"Joey Donovan Guido's new book on 'Holistic Online Marketing' seems deceptively simple comprising three sections on Foundation, Your Website, and Your Blog; plus a great section on Social Media. But don't let the simplicity and clarity of excellent writing and editing fool you — the book puts together the fundamentals in a powerful way starting with the 'Doctor Analogy' (you need to assess and work on the total 'patient').

Then there's the excellent formula of attending to SEO, UX, plus Conversions on your website (each have a chapter). Should your blogs convert visitors to prospects? While most of us focus on using blogs for content marketing, Guido advises that you are building relationships on your blog … and this can and does lead to conversions. That's an important nuance and the book is filled with them — excellent for newbies, clients, and even experienced publishing teams. Don't miss the section on conversions on LinkedIn."
— *Scott Frangos, Founder and Chief Optimizer for Webdirexion LLC, the digital marketing agency*

"*A Holistic Guide to Online Marketing* is an insightful and accessible book. Author Joey Donovan Guido demystifies the often-opaque realm of SEO with fun and humorous analogies. He smoothly integrates SEO best practices into a useful discussion of user experience and conversion.

Guido introduces readers to user experience (UX) with stories from the real world, what he calls 'analog UX.' These concrete examples make UX an accessible topic for business owners and decision makers who need and want to learn more about this critical domain."
— *Eric Olive, Founder and Lead Trainer at UI UX Training*

A Holistic Guide to Online Marketing

A Holistic Guide
to
Online Marketing
SEO • User Experience • Conversion

Joey Donovan Guido

Cuppa SEO Press

A Holistic Guide to Online Marketing:
SEO, User Experience, Conversion

Cuppa SEO Press • www.joeydonovanguido.com

ISBN: 978-1-7331952-0-1

To Kara, Max, Joss, Sheila, Skye and Olivia —
Thank you for helping me become my true self, and for your unwavering support throughout my life (including the writing of this book).

ACKNOWLEDGEMENTS

To Eric Olive, Kathleen Watson and Jon Wuebben, who have been instrumental in the creation of this book.

To Grandma Frances, I still think about you every day.

Editors:	Kathleen Watson
	Eric Olive
Formatter:	Robert Rubin
Cover Design:	Hannah Sandvold
	Joey Donovan Guido
Font:	Open Sans

Contents

PUTTING THE PIECES TOGETHER

Many Pieces Make Up the Whole

THE DOCTOR ANALOGY
What would you think if you went to the doctor for your annual physical, and he or she checked only your right arm and your left foot?

That's not a full physical, right? There's a lot more that needs to be done to make sure you're functioning properly — as a whole.

It's the same with online marketing. It has to be looked at holistically, as one.

Yet most of the time, this is not the case. Instead, each facet of online marketing is often addressed in a silo, disassociated from the rest. The result can be fractured and ineffective online initiatives that leave organizations feeling frustrated.

To achieve the greatest success with your efforts, you need to take a step back and look at the entire online marketing process from a global perspective ...

THE GLOBAL VIEW
First, identify the correct order for your efforts so you know what to work on first, second, third and so on. When new clients contact me, the first thing they often say is, "I need help with my social media." My response to this is always the same. I encourage the client to take a step back and work with me to formulate a global view of their business. What's working? What's not? Do they have a website? A blog?

As you'll see, having a social media presence is NOT the first order of business. Nor is it the second. It actually comes AFTER you've gotten your website and blog in order.

Why? Think about it. If you don't have a solid website and blog, where are you going to drive your Facebook and LinkedIn followers? Most likely, to SOMEBODY ELSE'S CONTENT! This doesn't help you build relationships. Instead, it makes you a messenger — delivering somebody else's content to YOUR readers.

The order in which you need to roll out your online marketing initiatives is a critical component to *A Holistic Guide to Online Marketing*. Here's what that exact order looks like as it's broken down in each part of the book:

PART 1: THE FOUNDATION
Gaining an understanding of search engine optimization (SEO), user experience (UX) and conversion (CV) — and why they're important to your online success.

Before you do any work with your online marketing, you'll need to gain a clear understanding of search engine optimization, user experience and conversion. Because there's so much confusion around each of these strategies, this book begins with an in-depth chapter on each.

You'll get a solid understanding of what each strategy is and why it's important before we address how to use each strategy on your website, blog and social media efforts.

Without a good understanding of the foundation, your online efforts will not be as successful as they could be. Remember, making a change for the sake of change is like playing darts with a blindfold on after being spun around until you're dizzy. In other words, it's very unscientific, and very unreliable. You might hit the target, or somebody might get hurt!

When you understand the foundation of online marketing, you can "take aim" and make deliberate changes. And because you know exactly what you did and why you did it, if it was successful, you can replicate the process again and again. And if it wasn't so successful, you know which changes you might want to test going forward.

So resist the urge to skip ahead. Instead, read the chapters on SEO, UX and conversion before diving deeper into the book.

PART 2: YOUR WEBSITE
Next, you'll apply these learnings to your website, optimizing every nook and cranny with solid SEO, UX and conversion strategies.

The SEO will help you get found, the UX will keep your visitors comfortable and happy while they're on your site, and your conversion strategy will help them take the next step you'd like them to take.

When it comes to online marketing, address your website BEFORE your work on any other platform. Why? Because it's your virtual hub — your linchpin — that everything else revolves around. Part 2 of *A Holistic Guide to Online Marketing* is all about how to effectively implement intelligent SEO, UX and conversion strategies into your website — both desktop and mobile versions — respectively.

PART 3: YOUR BLOG
Once your website has been addressed for SEO, UX and conversion, the next step is to learn how to apply these strategies to your blog.

And although some of the applications are quite similar, others are radically different.

Before we discuss these strategies, we'll take an in-depth look into the world of blogging, addressing topics such as:

- Defining the purpose of your blog
- How to write a blog post
- The three C's of writing awesome blog titles
- What are tags & categories
- Blog post frequency & length
- Original content vs. duplicate content
- Scheduling posts
- Blog campaigns
- The role of social media in blogging (a prelude to Part 4)

PART 4: SOCIAL MEDIA

Now that your blog is up and running (yay!), it's finally time to learn how to apply SEO, UX and conversion into your social media.

As mentioned earlier, before you start publishing content on social media, you've got to have something to say AND have a place of your own to say it.

By this point, your blog and website are both optimized, chock-full of rich and relevant content, and contain solid UX and conversion strategies. Gone are the days of highlighting other people's content. Now you get to highlight your own!

As you may have guessed, social media needs SEO, UX and conversion strategies, too. We'll examine how to effectively apply these strategies to your Facebook, LinkedIn and Google My Business posts, respectively. We'll also take a step-by-step approach to optimizing each of these social media platforms, helping you stand head and shoulders above your competition.

In this section, we'll take a look at the "two sides" of social media: the human-facing side (LinkedIn, Facebook, Pinterest, etc.) and the SEO side (Google My Business). Understanding the differences between the two, and how to take full advantage of each side, plays a big role in your overall online marketing success.

Ready to begin? Then turn the page and get to know SEO ...

PART 1: THE FOUNDATION

Gaining an understanding of search engine optimization (SEO), user experience (UX) and conversion (CV) — and why they're important to your online success.

1. What is Search Engine Optimization (SEO)?

Your holistic guide to online marketing begins with SEO. In a nutshell, SEO is a process that has the ability to improve the natural ranking of your website or blog in search results — leading to increased traffic, sales, customer engagement and overall growth. SEO is the connector between someone who's making a specific query on Google (or another search engine) with websites and/or blogs that contain relevant information pertaining to the query.

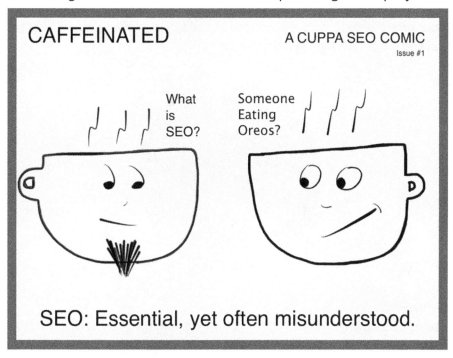

We've all performed countless searches, right? And on the surface, it seems pretty simple. Someone performs a search — say with the keyword "plumber" — and Google looks for and delivers results that are relevant to this keyword phrase. This, in and of itself, is no big news. But the question is, how does Google decide which results to list? And why do some sites or blogs rank higher than others?

Search engine optimization is a large part of the answer to these questions. It plays a critical role in determining where a website or blog ranks in the natural (also referred to as "organic") search results.

Let's take a deeper look at how this works, and learn about ...

THE SEO PIE

Part of search engine optimization is the selection and strategic implementation of optimal keywords into your website content. Keywords account for approximately one-third of the SEO pie — a significant amount, for sure, but not a complete package by any means. In the past, keywords were a bigger piece of the pie. Then blogs and social media came along.

Now, effective SEO is broken into three major parts: keywords, content and social media. Together, they make up the SEO pie.

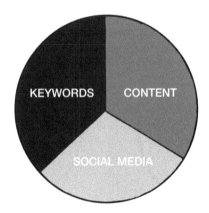

1. Keywords

You've probably heard the term "keywords" referred to more than once in relation to your website. And although you may know they're a critical element in SEO, you may be wondering exactly what keywords are. Let's take a look!

Keywords are terms or phrases that, when implemented into your website, can help connect you with people who are looking for what you do. In other words, when the keywords you use on your site are in alignment with the search terms people use to find the specific products or services you offer, there's a better chance Google will present your website higher in the search results.

For example, if you were a dentist in Los Angeles, CA, phrases like "Dentist," and "Dentist Los Angeles" would be good keywords because they're actually terms people use to find a dentist in Los Angeles, CA.

That said, the quality of your keywords makes a big difference in how effective they are. Many factors go into determining which keywords are best for your website and blog, including:

- The size of your site
- How long it's been around
- How many people are searching for a specific keyword phrase within the region(s) where you do business
- How much competition you'll be facing for that particular keyword or keyword phrase
- How relevant a keyword phrase is for your business or organization

Now that we've got a basic definition in place, let's dive deeper for a greater understanding of keywords.

Keyword Hierarchy

Let's start with what I call "keyword hierarchy," something I've developed over the years to help identify optimal keyword (and keyword phrase) usage.

Essentially, when optimizing content, you don't want to have just one keyword phrase that you hammer on ad nauseam. Instead, you'll want to create a well-rounded list of keyword phrases for every web page and blog post. Depending on the topic and the content length, this list could include 3–5 keyword phrases or more than a dozen.

No matter the length of the list, make sure every single phrase is relevant to the topic, service or product you "discuss" in your content. Some call this "topic-based SEO," among other things, but I just call it good writing. For instance, if you have a pet food store that caters to dogs, well-written copy won't be limited to dog food. You'll want to talk about food for puppies as well as for older dogs ... about different breeds of dogs and what foods might be best for them ... and don't forget dog treats! You might even want to cover how the foods you sell affect not only canine general health, but also canine dental health. You get the idea. Well-rounded keyword usage helps produce well-rounded content that's good for the human eye — and for SEO.

Primary, Secondary & Semantic Keywords

Once you've developed your list of keywords for a particular web page or blog post, you'll need to decide which are primary, secondary and semantic, respectively.

- Primary Keywords: As "primary" indicates, these are the main keywords in your content. Sometimes you'll determine them in advance; other times your organically written content will dictate them.
- Secondary Keywords: Used less often than primary keywords, these are still specific to the website page or blog post you're optimizing.
- Semantic Keywords: Used only once or twice at most, these still play an important role in "rounding out" the relevance of the content.

As you can see, semantic and secondary keywords play a supporting role in the optimization of content. They're good to use, but they don't have the oomph that a main keyword has, typically for three reasons: 1) they have low search numbers; 2) they have high competition; 3) they're not the main topic of the page, but they work tangentially to support the main topic. An SEO novice might use secondary and semantic keywords as main keywords — or might overlook them completely. In Part 2 of the book, we'll dive deeper into primary, secondary and semantic keyword usage.

Long-tail Keywords

This is a fancy term for using keyword phrases that are typically three or more words long. Very often, what makes a keyword phrase long-tail is the fact that it has some "definers" or "qualifiers" in it, making it very specific.

For example, "dentist" is most likely going to be a strong keyword, no matter where your dental office is located. But I'll bet it also has very high competition. Adding qualifiers to the keyword — "Dentist Madison WI" for example — makes it more specific and might have less competition from other area dental offices.

Case Study — First Choice Dental
First Choice Dental (FCD) is a local dental chain in Dane County, WI. In our work together, Cuppa SEO optimized dozens of First Choice Dental's website pages and blog posts. Part of this optimization included implementing long-tail keywords in exactly the way I described above.

Take a look at the actual numbers (as of this writing), and you'll see that the long-tail keyword is preferred over the short-tail keyword:

Keyword Phrase	Monthly Search in Madison WI	Competition	FCD Rank
Dentist	1,000	High	2nd on page 1
Dentist Madison WI	880	Medium	1st on page 1

As you can see, FCD ranks well on Google's natural search results for both phrases, but it ranks better for the long-tail keyword: It's easier to crush weaker competition!

A nice thing about long-tail keywords is that they often contain multiple short-tail keywords. In the example above, "Dentist Madison WI" actually contains, "Dentist," "Dentist Madison," and "Dentist Madison WI," so it really packs a punch.

Keyword Density
The term "keyword density" is worth a quick mention here. Keyword density is what it sounds like: the number of times (density) a keyword phrase appears on a page compared with the total number of words on the page.

Over the years, I've heard SEO experts argue that a keyword phrase needs to occur a certain percentage of the time to be considered an actual keyword. Through testing, I've found this untrue. Although a keyword phrase typically needs to appear more than once within the content to be taken seriously by Google, it DOES NOT need to appear a certain percentage of the time. That's no way to optimize — and that's no way to write good, relevant content. In Part 2 of this book, we'll take a step-by-step look at exactly *where* to implement your keywords, which is a critical component of solid SEO practices.

Another point of view is that it's *context* — not keyword occurrence rate — that's important. As you might have guessed, I agree that *context* is extremely important. When you're writing rich, relevant, helpful content, that's a third of the SEO pie. Of course, for content to meet all of these requirements, it has to make sense within the context of the page it's on as well as within the website or blog as a whole. Let's talk a bit more about content ...

2. Content

In plain terms, content is the copy (words) and imagery found on your website and blog. And, when it comes to content and SEO, there are two important factors to keep in mind.

The Relevance Factor

Just like a human, Google is judging your content and determining whether it's rich and relevant or boring and "thin." Rich, relevant content helps each of your web pages and blog posts gain more authority in Google's eyes, which means ranking higher in search results. It also increases credibility and engagement with actual *people*, too.

Thin content accomplishes the opposite, and it might lead your website or blog toward what I call the "black hole of Google Panda" — never to be found in organic search results. The good news is that if you take the time to create quality content, your site is already partially optimized!

The Freshness Factor

Freshness is an important factor in how well your website ranks in natural search results on Google. But *where* you add that fresh content to your site is just as important as how rich, relevant and useful it is.

Many novice SEO practitioners will tell you that the best way to inject new content into your site is to "freshen up" your homepage and subpages with new copy and keywords — sometimes on a monthly basis.

Taking this approach on a well-optimized site will most likely backfire.

Why? Because once your site is well optimized, changing the SEO on your homepage or subpages is similar to changing your phone number every month: It makes no sense. Just as your customers depend on your phone number as a means to reach you, Google is depending on your optimized content to find you and connect you with individuals who need you. Once you change the SEO on a page, the result can often be going back to square one — losing some or all of your page authority (credibility) with Google.

In other words, unless something changes — like a service or product — or one of your pages starts to perform poorly, you'll want to leave well-optimized content alone on your home page and subpages.

So, if you need fresh content, where does it come from?

Fresh Content Comes from Your Blog
Use that blog of yours to generate the fresh content Google — and your viewers — are looking for. Adding a minimum of one blog post per week can do wonders for your "freshness factor." Why? Because every time you publish a blog post, Google notices and gives your website credit for having some new, fresh content.

And, by the way, each blog post is excellent fodder for your social media efforts, too. Speaking of which, let's review ...

3. Social Media
Your social media efforts round out the SEO pie. Just as with your website and blog, you'll want to optimize each and every social media post you publish. This means you'll want to incorporate relevant keywords into each post.

It's important to note that platforms such as Facebook, LinkedIn and Twitter can help with business growth and relationship development, but it's Google My Business that holds the lion's share of SEO value in the world of social media.

In other words, consistently publishing posts through your Google My Business page can play a significant role in boosting your overall online authority. Google has made itself extremely self-important in the social media world. Like it or not, Google My Business is an extremely critical platform in the SEO equation. My advice: Use it to your advantage.

At this moment, you might be feeling the urge to jump ahead to Part 4 of this book and begin implementing all of the social media optimization strategies. Resist the urge! Remember, your online marketing will be most effective if you stay true to implementing the strategies in this book in the order they're presented.

SEO Pie Recap

Addressing all parts of the SEO pie helps Google identify what you do, so when an individual searches for your services or products, you'll more likely show up closer to the top in natural search results as Cuppa SEO does in the following example. The better optimized your website, blog and social media efforts, the better chance you have of ranking high in these search results, which look like this ...

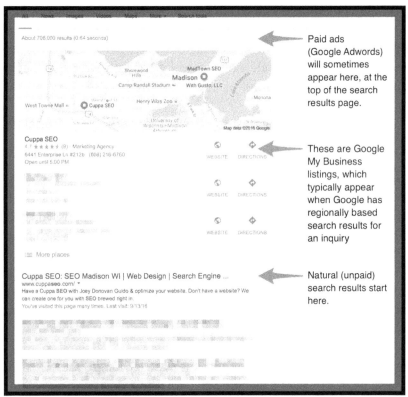

Paid ads (Google Adwords) will sometimes appear here, at the top of the search results page.

These are Google My Business listings, which typically appear when Google has regionally based search results for an inquiry

Natural (unpaid) search results start here.

Holistic Side Note: *Throughout this book, we'll be referring to Google as our primary search engine. The reason is simple: Google is king of all search engines. But don't worry about the others, because the strategies we're discussing here apply to all search engines.*

THE RAFT ANALOGY

Getting your website to appear at the top of search results can be compared to how a raft works. Let me explain …

Imagine that you're embarking on a whitewater rafting expedition. You and five fellow adventurers are ready to brave the rapids — and probably get soaking wet!

What would happen if you took your un-inflated raft out of your car and threw it in the water? It would sink, right?

Before you get into your raft, you have to pump it up to the optimal number of pounds per square inch (PSI). With every pump of air, your raft comes closer to its optimal PSI, which makes the raft more and more *buoyant.*

Half pumped, some parts would probably be above water and others below, but the raft would not yet be ready to bear any weight. Once you've attained the optimal PSI, the entire raft will sit on the surface of the water — even with six people in it!

Your website, metaphorically speaking, is similar to a raft. It needs to be "pumped up" before it can rise to the top. But instead of air being the catalyst to bring it to the surface, your SEO efforts help your website become more buoyant.

Every well-optimized web page and blog post is like a pump of air into that raft, assisting with your website's "buoyancy factor." The same is true for your social media efforts. Every optimized social platform, and every optimized post, is like a pump of air that improves the "PSI" of your website. As mentioned earlier, Google My Business is going to be the most influential channel for SEO value.

In Part 2 of this book, we'll be examining the many facets of a successful website. We'll lead the discussion by reviewing a step-by-step process for implementing SEO into every nook and cranny of your site. From creating a killer keyword report, to defining exactly where you need to implement SEO, you'll learn how to increase the buoyancy of your site for better visibility.

Part 2 will also address user experience (UX) and conversion strategies for your website. Speaking of UX, it just happens to be our next chapter. Ready to dive in?

2. What is User Experience (UX)?

UX is something that occurs during every interaction you have with customers and potential customers, both online and in the "analog" world. It's the positive, negative or neutral reaction a visitor has with your brand online or in person.

The user experience often determines whether or not someone chooses your service, your product or signs up for one of your offers.

When the UX is good, a visitor will stick around and even look forward to coming back to your site. In a way, good UX is similar to going to your favorite restaurant where you love the food, the wait staff and the atmosphere.

UX exists everywhere, but there are two main types of UX:

ANALOG USER EXPERIENCE (AUX)
Analog user experiences occur all around us in the real world: At a restaurant, a supermarket, a gas station, where we work, and so on. We have user experiences with products we buy, starting with product packaging design and instructions for use.

When you get into your car, you have a user experience whether you're conscious of it or not. Every button, every dial, steering wheel placement, seat comfort, etc., all contribute to a positive, negative or neutral AUX.

An AUX can also occur between people; in other words, it can be based on a human relationship.

It's easy to forget that before there were computers and mobile devices, most of an organization's user experience took place in the analog world, either face-to-face, over the phone, through the mail or (gasp!) even in print catalogs.

Holistic Side Note: Although Analog User Experience is a term I coined, the concepts laid out in this section overlap with other disciplines — specifically human factors and service design.

DIGITAL USER EXPERIENCE
Digital user experiences occur, as you might have guessed, online through websites, blogs, social media and email. There are other forms of Digital User Experiences such as TV, Nintendo (if you're my son, Max), music, etc., but we won't be concerned with them in this book.

Consider that all of these digital user experiences are still tied, to a degree, to the analog world through the devices you use to access a product or service via the digital content made available to you.

A large part of Cuppa SEO's web design process focuses on the creation of a positive user experience on every website we build. That's why Part 2 of this book is chock-full of real-world examples of both good and bad website UX. In fact, we'll be dissecting many website pages (on both desktop and mobile) to clarify what a good and bad user experience looks like. Examples help you begin to see your own website from a new perspective, leading you on a path to an improved UX for your visitors.

Until then, let's get better acquainted with UX through a handful of true stories from the analog world. As you'll see, every Analog UX holds within it many treasures that can be applied to the digital world of your website.

MY FAMILY ROAD TRIP & THE ANALOG USER EXPERIENCE
PART 1: HILTON GARDEN INN

During the last week of a summer not long ago, my family took a road trip from the Midwest to New York. We stopped at some interesting places along the way. In addition to spending lots of time with my wife and sons, the trip offered a variety of observations in real-world (analog) user experience.

You might be wondering why a company that specializes in web design, blogging and search engine optimization would be talking about analog user experience. The reason is simple: The core principle of both analog and digital user experience is the same: to give each person who visits the best possible experience.

In this series, we'll be exploring mini case studies in AUX that can be applied to your business and your website.

Let's begin with the first hotel we stayed at on our way to NYC — the Hilton Garden Inn, in Cleveland, Ohio.

On the trip to NY, it was just me and the boys (my wife flew out ahead of us), and we were exhausted from a long day of driving.

When we arrived at the hotel, I was informed that I'd be billed $16 for on-site parking. It wasn't a big deal, but it was a surprise all the same.

Our room contained many unique attributes I had never experienced in a hotel, including:

- A knot of long hair on the bathroom floor
- A rickety toilet that teetered from side to side
- A rusty toilet paper holder that was half detached from the wall
- An ancient-looking shower that was built with absolutely NO design sense

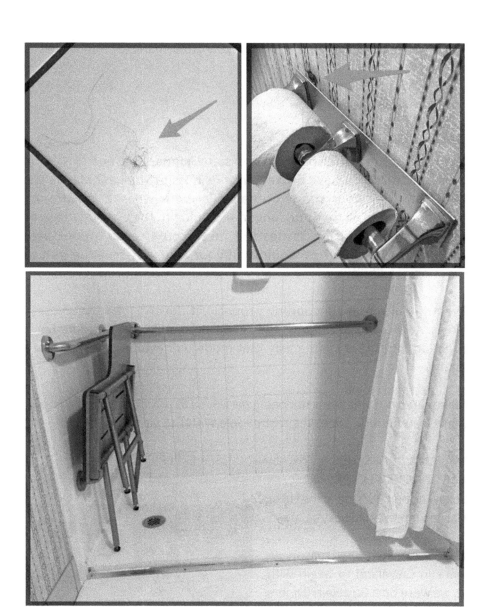

In addition, none of the vending machines had water, and the jacuzzi (which my kids love for some reason) was not clean.

Overall, my 9-year old son, Joss, gave this hotel 1.5 out of 5 stars.

The hotel's branding clearly states, "Welcome to the Hilton Garden Inn, home of the EXCELLENT stay. Excellence drives us!"

There was nothing excellent about our stay other than the relief we felt as we left the hotel.

The user experience was horrible!

How this Relates to Your Website

Is your website suffering from the same kinds of issues this hotel presented? Do you have broken links or missing images? Maybe the information on your site is outdated, or your website is suffering from an old design that's no longer appealing to the eye. Maybe your navigation is confusing. Issues like these could cause a poor user experience, which in turn could cost your company revenue (not to mention credibility).

Even if your site is functioning properly, it doesn't mean your users like it. At the end of the day, the hotel room still performed its basic function, but it did so in a way that made us never want to go there again.

Make sure your website is not being perceived as a yucky hair ball. Instead, make it something appealing that people WANT to visit again.

MY FAMILY ROAD TRIP & THE ANALOG USER EXPERIENCE
PART 2: LUCKY'S CAFE

Following our first stop at the Hilton Garden Inn, we hit Lucky's Cafe.

Lucky's was the real reason we were in Cleveland to begin with, as we were on a Guy Fieiri (Diners, Drive-Ins & Dives) road trip as we made our way to New York.

The analog user experience my boys and I had while visiting the cafe was a different story.

Lucky's had a lot going for it.

Here's a partial list us guys pulled together:

- Before we even walked in, the aesthetic of the building and the outside dining area were impressive and inviting.
- Inside, the beautiful aesthetic continued with a clean, fresh rustic design that was warm and homey. From color palette to furniture and overall decor, it was well designed.
- Freshly baked pastries adorned the counter near the entrance.

- The wait staff was friendly, informative, authentic and compassionate (I have some dietary restrictions that they were extremely willing to cater to without any hassle).
- The food was made from scratch: no shipping in bread or jam — or the goodies on the treats counter. They created everything themselves — and everything was delicious!
- Lucky's has great relationships in the Cleveland community, partnering with farmers, butchers and gardeners who provide the restaurant with local ingredients.

- The menu was minimalist, the choices mouthwatering; it made options clear and easy to understand.
- The food was awesome — fresh, delicious and beautifully plated.

Note: Our server graciously joined us for a photo.

My son Joss gave Lucky's Cafe a 5 out of 5 for analog user experience, although I think he'd rather fly than drive to get there next time.

How this Relates to Your Website

In each installment of our analog user experience series, we'll look at ways our real-world experiences relate to your website's online user experiences.

Aesthetic

How does the exterior of Lucky's compare to the homepage of your website? There's a good chance that visitors will land on your homepage first, and it needs to impress. The same can be said about your subpages, which are like the inside of Lucky's. If your subpages are confusing, bland or hard to navigate, your user experience score will plummet.

Content

The food at Lucky's was made from scratch by staff. The same should be true of your website content. It needs to be original, created from scratch by you (or a professional writer) so it's unique and relevant. Of course, every nook and cranny of your content should be optimized with SEO.

The freshness factor comes into critical play with your blog, which is the easiest way to continually integrate fresh content into your website. In a way, fresh blog content is like the treat counter at Lucky's, because fresh content is as appealing to Google's algorithm as fresh pastries are to human taste buds.

Conversion

To achieve high conversion on your website, your call-to-action needs to be clear. Notice that I said "call-to-action," not "calls-to-action." Too often, websites offer way too many calls-to-action to customers (bad for UX), when they should be providing only one or two. Lucky's menu is the perfect metaphorical example of a successful call-to-action. It's clear, easy to understand, and it wasn't multiple pages long like the menus we've all had to fumble through at a cafe or diner.

When we offer only one or two calls-to-action, we wind up providing a better user experience, and we in turn have a greater chance of having the customer — the site visitor — take action.

In other words, avoid this ...

And if you're ever in Cleveland, Ohio, be sure to visit Lucky's Cafe!

MY FAMILY ROAD TRIP & THE ANALOG USER EXPERIENCE
PART 3: JUAN'S FOOD CART
Next on our road trip to New York was ... New York! We stayed in the heart of the city on 43rd Street and 9th Avenue.

Little did I know that amidst all the traffic, noise and hustle, I'd find one truly excellent analog user experience from a gentleman named Juan who owned the food cart on the corner.

As a friendly New Yorker myself, I started having conversations with Juan each day, which he seemed to appreciate as much as I did. Because I was so impressed, I wanted to share ...

The Details of My Analog User Experience
From the moment I approached Juan's Food Cart, he was friendly and approachable. Even though he was busy with a line of people, he made me feel like a friend.

- Juan and his wife took our order each day and cooked everything fresh, right in front of us.
- Although they were cooped up in a tiny food cart, there was a friendly, positive vibe coming from this small business. It was obvious they loved what they did, and they loved each other, which made me WANT to spend my money there.
- The food was great — fresh, hot and made to order.
- The price? $3 for each bacon, egg and cheese sandwich on a Kaiser roll.
- He gave us free stuff — even though there was nothing in it for him. Juan and his wife seemed so appreciative to have our brief conversations that they started giving us free treats each day. I was so impressed to see such a good-hearted gesture.
- I looked forward to seeing Juan and his wife each morning.

How this Relates to Your Website & Your Business

Approachability
Is your website or your storefront as approachable as Juan's? It doesn't matter if it's a food cart or a Ferrari dealership. Friendly service goes a long way toward building trust and making customers feel at home.

Finding the Right Solution for Each Client
From a global view, Juan listened to what my needs were and delivered exactly what I asked for. He didn't try to upsell, supersize or add extra dollars to his pocket by pushing me to buy more. In a way, this is a simplistic view of delivering custom solutions. For many of us, solutions are much more nuanced and complicated than: "egg over easy, with bacon and cheese on a Kaiser roll," but Juan had the service concept mastered — specifically, what does the customer need, and how can I best meet that need?

Exceeding Expectations
From delivering an excellent meal, to free treats and better service than many fancy restaurants, Juan's service exceeded my expectations.

A word on free: Juan provides an excellent example of giving something of value at no charge. I'm not saying you should give away products or services, but there is something every business can offer with no strings attached: valuable content. Whether it's a blog, webinar, workshop or infographic, delivering useful information to clients and potential clients can go a long way when it comes to building trust, raising credibility and positioning you as an authority in your industry. And in today's content-marketing age, it's also a necessity if you want to grow your business.

Price
The one thing I had trouble wrapping my head around was why Juan charged so little for a fresh meal. My wife, Kara, pointed out that Juan's Food Cart had a lot of closeby competition, and the price point was probably where he needed to be if he wanted to remain a relevant choice for his customers.

You can debate this, as better service can often warrant higher prices because the perceived value of the product is heightened by the service that surrounds it. Of course, if you've done your homework and clearly defined your customer demographic, you should have a good idea of where your price "tops off" before it becomes unacceptable to customers. Juan seemed like a smart guy, so I'm not questioning his business tactics. On the contrary, taking his lead and determining the right price for your products or services is always a good idea.

If you're ever at 43rd Street and 9th Avenue in New York, be sure to stop by Juan's Food Cart for breakfast.

MY FAMILY ROAD TRIP & THE ANALOG USER EXPERIENCE
PART 4: THE WAFFLE HOUSE
On the first leg of our road trip home from New York, we got hungry in Ohio.

Although one of Cuppa SEO's web designers knows Ohio like the back of his hand (he's from West Liberty, Ohio), we had no tips from him about where to eat. With the help of a Google search, we found a Dunkin' Donuts and a Waffle House close to each other.

Considering that the Waffle House might offer greater menu variety and food that might be a little healthier, that's where we ended up. And although it was an interesting analog user experience, it was not a pleasant one.

From the parking lot, everything seemed fine ... and then we entered the restaurant. It was freezing! It must have been between 30 and 40 degrees.

We spoke with the server about it, and she explained that during her employee-orientation process, she learned that the directive from leadership was to "get people in and out in 20 minutes or less," because they "didn't want people getting comfortable and hanging around." Waffle House apparently keeps the thermostat low in its restaurants to encourage people to "eat and run." Employees aren't allowed to adjust the temperature, so many of them wear three layers of clothing to work.

Other aspects that made this a poor analog user experience included a mistake in my younger son's order, and all patrons being exposed to the incessant chatter of wait staff about their personal lives.

We read with interest a prominent message on the menu from the leadership team: It is Waffle House's goal to deliver a great experience where everyone is treated with "courtesy, fairness and respect."

Maybe their customer demographic is penguins?

The philosophy on Waffle House collateral told a very different story from the experience of both the internal and external customer. From what I'm told, most Waffle Houses are not like this. In fact, after posting an article about this on my Cuppa SEO blog, many die-hard Waffle House aficionados told me of excellent experiences they've had. My family didn't dine at one of those Waffle Houses, so let's take a look at ...

How this Relates to Your Website & Your Business Overall
The worst part of our experience wasn't the cold; it was the fact that Waffle House messaging made it all about *them*.

It wasn't about the customer experience, the best crispy bacon in town or the server who gave just the right amount of attention. It was a transaction, one which had no meaning other than monetary gain.

It was all about volume — about making the greatest amount of profit possible, which was made evident in the purposeful desire to cause discomfort by "freezing out" customers.

To avoid giving customers a "Waffle House Experience," it's important for all of us to ask the following questions about our website AND our in-person interactions:

Is my website about my customer, or is it about me? If it's not customer-facing, it needs to change.

- Am I addressing customer pain points and needs, or am I telling them how great I am?
- Am I showing customers how my products or services can help them? Or am I just asking them to buy?
- What can I do to make people *want* to spend time on my website? Do I have a single, clear call-to-action for them to follow on each page? Is the content on my pages, and on my blog, chock-full of relevant information that's actually helpful?
- Am I developing relationships with customers?

To this last point, are my employees following a customer-centric philosophy, or are they me-centric?

In some businesses, commission structures can make it difficult for employees to look at a customer as a whole person, as opposed to seeing them simply as a sale.

One of the greatest customer-facing philosophies I've seen and been a part of is Apple. Why? Because when a customer enters an Apple store, it is never about how much you can sell — it is about understanding who the customers are, what they need and then offering the very best solution possible.

Whether your business model is trying to make a $50 million annual revenue quota, or whether it's simply trying to make sure there's enough income to pay the bills and your team, it can be easy to start perceiving people — your customers — as things that need to be moved through a funnel.

And although the funnel analogy is excellent for analyzing your processes, once people are no longer looked at as individuals, your company runs the risk of becoming me-centric. Avoid this narcissistic trap by always making it about your customers. They'll appreciate it, they'll tell their friends and colleagues — and most importantly, they'll never have to worry about freezing their butts off in your office or retail store!

ANALOG USER EXPERIENCE: THE CASE OF THE MISSING HOT DOG

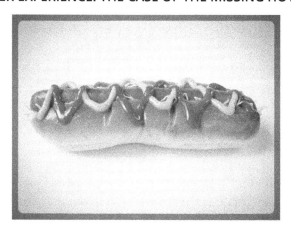

What happened to the eighth hot dog?

I found myself asking this question over and over during a recent supermarket shopping excursion.

When I went to pick up a package of hot dogs for dinner, I noticed there were only seven. Inspecting a few other brands, I noticed the same.

This may sound like a trivial observation, but when you're part of a family of four (plus our pesky cat), you're kind of depending on having two hot dogs per person.

After all, hot dog buns are packaged as eight.

Somebody had to decide to make this change — but why?

Did customer feedback tell a tale of one too many hot dogs? Or did the price of producing hot dogs go up (at least for the more-premium offerings), causing these companies to cut out some of the product instead of increasing the price? Or was there simply a desire for more profit per pack?

No matter the reason, my user experience — my UX — was poor. And I can't be the only one.

Why am I talking about this here? This analog user experience raises a question that's relevant to web design and your website ...

How this Relates to Your Website & Your Business

Addressing Customer Needs
Are you addressing your customers' needs with your products and services? Or are you trying to fit them into a box that's convenient for you?

The Apple watch is a great example. Apple limits your band color selection to how it wants to pair the band with the timepiece. Using the Sport model as an example, if you want a black watch with a black band, no problem. If you want a silver watch with a black band (a popular and classic combo, if I do say so myself), you're out of luck ... almost. You can choose to pay an extra $50 and get a black band as an accessory. This might be good for Apple and its bottom line, but it's a bad UX for customers — and it's in direct conflict with Apple's fantastic customer-facing philosophy we talked about in our Waffle House example just a few pages ago.

Are You Addressing Integrations?
Integration is the process of making it possible to use (integrate) one app with another, completely different app. Integrations are gaining prevalence. The makers of WordPress, Drupal, Salesforce, Slack, Meister Task, MailChimp and many others understand that their customers need apps created by other vendors to work harmoniously with their own.

In the case of the missing hot dog, how does a 7-pack of franks work with my 8-pack of buns? It used to work seamlessly, *but now there's a gap* — and that gap means lost money to the customer. In this case, I'm paying for an extra bun. Plus I'm still paying for what used to be eight hot dogs, which means *the value proposition of the product has actually gone down.*

The Role of Packaging

Just as hot dogs are packaged, your website, too, is packaged. The way it looks and functions matters to those who visit your site. If it's non-responsive and non-mobile-friendly, both Google and your visitors are going to notice.

Consider the blister pack. You know what I mean — those confounding plastic packages that are nearly impossible to open without the risk of inflicting bodily injury. Don't let your website be a blister pack. Make it responsive and mobile-friendly. Even better, make it easy to use with a clear navigational hierarchy — and make it attractive! All of this adds up to a good user experience.

Once you've created a good UX on your site, don't make your visitors think about what they need to do next. Give them a clear, compelling call-to-action — most likely a button — near the top of the page so it's easy for them to take the next step. Master this basic conversion strategy.

Now imagine for moment that you've accomplished everything mentioned in the last two paragraphs. Your website would now be a well-designed, easy-open package.

At first glance, these may seem like trivial things to focus on. But they're not. Every single piece of your product, service, or web design moves someone toward a positive or negative user experience. One "little" problem may be the tipping point that makes someone disengage.

3. What is Conversion (CV)?

Now that we've got visitors feeling good about where they've arrived, we need a solid conversion strategy to ensure that they know exactly what to do next. Whether it's filling out a contact form, giving you a call, or downloading some complimentary content, well-designed conversion strategies make next steps easy and crystal clear.

Conversion is an important part of any organization's long-term success. Yet conversion is often misunderstood. That's why it's part of this ridiculously thick (but hopefully informative) book.

A multitude of conversion strategies and practices exist, but for our purposes here, we'll be focusing on calls-to-action (CTAs).

We'll begin by defining conversion and discussing why it's an important strategy for your website, blog and social media.

Later in the book you'll find many more examples that clarify how to apply calls-to-action to your online marketing efforts. But for now it's all about having a solid understanding of what conversion is and why it's important.

CONVERSION DEFINED
Conversion is a strategy that takes a website, blog or social media visitor from where they are to where you want them to go.

Please note how I've worded this, *"from where they are, to where **you** want them to go."*

Before we go further, let me be clear that I am by no means suggesting that arm-twisting, manipulation, guilt, lies, deceit, fear-based methods — or any form of skullduggery — be used to lead your digital visitor in a particular direction.

What I am suggesting is that you need to assess and understand what the majority of your customers struggle with (their pain points), and then craft your conversion strategy based on that. In other words, the best way to get visitors to go where you want them to go is to make that destination a place that *solves their problem.* (Your services and/or products do solve problems, right?)

For example, let's say you operate a dental office, and a potential new patient lands on your website's homepage. If you're like any of the dental offices we've worked with over the years, you and your team have determined that the next step you'd like the visitor to take is to call you — which means your conversion strategy needs to be a call-to-action (CTA) that makes it easy for that potential new patient to call and make an appointment.

Most people don't schedule a dental appointment "just because." There's usually a reason. It might be pain, or the need for cleaning, or "the year is coming to an end and I haven't used up my allotted dental care dollars."

All of these reasons share a common thread: the need to make an appointment with a dentist. So in this case, your conversion strategy is based on this point.

CONVERSION ON YOUR WEBSITE
Solid website conversion makes it easy for a visitor to take the next step to become a customer or client. Important stuff, right?

More often than not, the conversion strategy on your website will take the form of a call-to-action, which typically takes the form of a button or a text link.

The more we address a visitor's pain points in a clear, compelling way, and the more our UX makes them feel comfortable with us, the easier it will be for them to convert.

In the case of the dental office example — whether it's on your homepage or a subpage — your call-to-action could be something like:

Need to schedule an appointment?

CALL NOW

This, of course, is a more generalized CTA. If you had a CTA on the Root Canal page, you could engage by saying something like:

Think you might need a root canal?
Please get in touch with us for a complimentary assessment. We'll determine the exact cause of your pain and discuss treatment options.

SCHEDULE AN APPOINTMENT

Regardless of the message, your call-to-action buttons need to be properly placed on both your desktop and mobile site, respectively. The reason I say "respectively" is because of the differential in screen size between a laptop or desktop computer versus a mobile phone or tablet.

Different-sized screens call for different solutions, which often go beyond simple responsive design. In other words, you need to honor the user experience for whatever device a visitor is using.

On a laptop, or even a tablet, a call-to-action could work well if placed on the hero shot (main image at the top of the page). On an iPhone, that same CTA needs to go somewhere different to be effective — not to mention to remain readable for a good user experience.

Before we take a look at a handful of examples, let's talk about point of conversion ...

POINT OF CONVERSION
The point of conversion is the moment your visitor is faced with a critical decision: Do I take action or not? Your CTA button is sitting there, begging to be clicked. If you've done a good job of leading your visitor to this point of conversion, you've greatly increased the chance that the person will indeed make a mini conversion (click the button). If you haven't done the work, there's a good chance the individual hasn't made it to a point of conversion.

Let's take a look at some of the preparation that can more effectively lead someone to a point of conversion.

Because we're talking about websites here, your first step is making sure your site is findable (SEO). Next is ensuring that your visitor feels comfortable and on solid footing when arriving on your site (UX). If you've accomplished these two major goals, you've opened the possibility to convert that visitor.

But that's not all. You also need …

A Clear Intention: What's Your #1 Goal?
There's nothing random about leading website visitors from where they are to where you want them to go. As you might imagine, it's quite the opposite, which means you need to have a clear intention of what you want your visitors to do when they land on your homepage, subpage, squeeze page or blog.

> **Holistic Side Note:** A "squeeze page" is a web page that's devoid of any and all non-pertinent information or services. It's an obvious, direct payoff to the CTA that leads to the page, and it's in line with a brand's identity. The reason we call them squeeze pages is that they're not a typical product or services page. Squeeze pages don't typically live in your navigation, so the only way to get to them is through clicking on a call-to-action — on either your website, social media, or paid advertising such as Adwords.

This clear intention can come only from identifying THE #1 THING you want your visitors to do after they've arrived on your site. Do you want them to call or email you? Shop? Your #1 thing should align nicely with your organizations #1 goal.

Going back to our dental office example — or any medical office for that matter — *the #1 goal (call-to-action) is often to get new or existing patients to call to make an appointment.*

In this case, does a giveaway such as a "Dental Health Mini-book" or a PDF of the "Top 10 Ways to Prevent Cavities" align with our #1 goal?

NO ... which means giveaways are not the optimal choice for a call-to-action.

But we see it all the time. Sign up for this, download that, watch our video. When a business uses this strategy correctly, the goal is to build a longer email list. Now IF, *and only if*, your primary goal is to build a big email list — again for a very specific reason — go ahead and focus on getting as many qualified emails as you can.

But if your #1 goal is to get more calls, don't offer me a free ebook!

Keeping your #1 goal in mind when creating your CTAs will help you be more focused. It also makes it easier for your team to fine-tune your visitor's journey to the point of conversion with content and imagery that's in complete alignment with your CTA (and your #1 goal) itself! Every step the visitor takes to the point of conversion needs to support the CTA. Even a slight disconnect can be fatal.

What's Your #2 Goal?
We often need a secondary #2 goal in case our visitor is not ready to take action on our #1 goal. A secondary goal can lead a visitor to take action on our #1 goal, but without that secondary, lead-up action, that visitor might not engage at all. Something like a video or free ebook might be a better step to prepare the visitor to act on #1.

Consider a real-world example of this philosophy, courtesy of the Dollar Shave Club homepage.

DOLLAR SHAVE CLUB EXAMPLE — HOMEPAGE
Here is one of my favorite examples of a website homepage. It's not my favorite because it's the most beautiful homepage I've ever seen, but it does do a beautiful job of seamlessly integrating UX and super-solid conversion. Let's examine why ...

#1 Goal

Dollar Shave Club's #1 goal is for visitors to buy razors as well as some of their other products. They do a great job of leading you to a point of conversion in just a few short words:

CTA Copy: "A great shave for a few bucks a month. No commitment. No fees. No BS."

Notice how Dollar Shave Club very clearly addresses multiple customer pain points: 1) the need for a great shave; 2) low cost; 3) no commitment; 4) no fees; 5) no BS ...

Button Copy: "DO IT"

And how the CTA button pays off the copy beautifully!

#2 Goal

The Dollar Shave Club also has a second CTA, which is the video. That leads us to the question ...

Why is the video there?

Think of it this way:

Your primary, #1 CTA is like a first date.
The person you're talking to is ready to take action: to go out to dinner. In the case of Dollar Shave Club, this represents the "DO IT" button — I'm ready to buy, get out of my way! I'm sick and tired of overpaying for razor blades, I'm busy — and I am psyched that my friend told me about Dollar Shave Club! Let's buy some blades!

Your secondary, #2 CTA is like the introduction.
"Hi, I'm James, nice to meet you. I live in California and I'm an architect ..."

The introduction is the part where you get to know someone enough to decide WHETHER OR NOT YOU WANT TO GO ON A FIRST DATE. The video accomplishes this: It helps us get to know Dollar Shave Club's personality, its products **and the benefits of its products** — with NO commitment at all. Is DCS for me or not? Watch the video and find out.

Solve a Problem: Make it About Them, Not You
This leads us to a good point ... making sure all of your CTAs are benefit-driven, which means they're clear about what problem(s) your products or services solve. Just as with your website and blog content, your calls-to-action need to solve problems or address a need.

Put yourself in your customers' shoes and determine what their pain points are. Once you identify those pain points, show them you can solve them with a *brief* call-to-action message that sits above or alongside your CTA button, just as in the Dollar Shave Club example above.

It's easy to get caught up in explaining the awesome process you have that makes your company unique. I could talk for hours about all of the nuances of SEO and how to apply optimized content into every nook and cranny of your website.

But *most people don't care*. If they're looking for an SEO expert, that means their website is probably not getting found enough (which is a pain point) and they need more organic traffic. Now if I say, "Cuppa SEO can help you get found on Google," I just let them know I can solve their problem — and I've told them in a succinct, easy-to-comprehend way.

If they're a tech geek like me, we can talk about details later. But they first need to know I can help ease or eliminate their pain.

DOLLAR SHAVE CLUB EXAMPLE — SUBPAGE
Sticking with Dollar Shave Club, let's examine the subpage for its razor selection. As we'll see, just as on the homepage, all of the content on this page is cohesive — meaning there's nothing extraneous or distracting. Every bit of information fully supports the point of conversion, a call-to-action that asks you to select your blade.

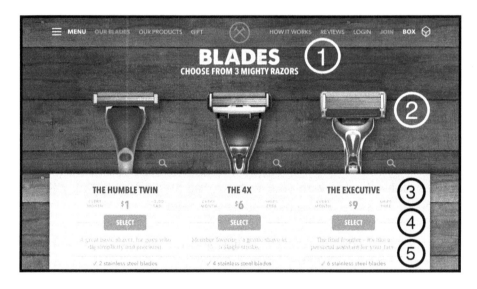

1. Headline and Subhead: Short, clear and a little playful, this headline lets you know EXACTLY where you are, and leads nicely to ...

2. Imagery: As the headline says, here are Dollar Shave Club's three blade options. Notice that just looking at them can tell you how "mighty" each one is and which is probably best for your beard (if you're a guy) or your legs (if you're a gal). Not much hair grows on the top of my head, but is it thick on my face (too bad it isn't the other way around)! Thanks to the imagery, I know — without having to read further — which blade I need (the executive, and it's not just because I'm a business owner).

    With this much clarity in the headline and imagery, there's a good chance the visitor is ready to jump to the point of conversion — which is why it's so important for those Select buttons to be present without needing to scroll to them.

3. Product Names and Price: The product names are just below the images. The names don't exist only for branding purposes; they further clarity the product, which strengthens the UX (keeping the visitor on solid ground). The price accomplishes this same goal and is also a payoff from what we saw on the homepage: "A great shave *for a few bucks a month*." Now, that's what I call a cohesive message that delivers what is promises!

4. The Point of Conversion: Here are our CTA buttons, simply marked "SELECT."

5. Additional Copy and Bullets: Notice that the CTAs live ABOVE the additional copy and bullets (which continue below the scroll line). This is deliberate and very well done, as enough information is present above the CTA for most visitors to make a decision to buy or not to buy.

   So, what's the remainder of the content for? Visitors who need more info — and for SEO.

Not every page has to have all five of these elements, but this is a fantastic example of how to set up a page for remarkable website conversion.

CONVERSION ON YOUR BLOG
A blog's main duty is NOT to convert someone on the spot. Quite the contrary, a blog is meant to help you *develop relationships*. For that reason, conversion works differently on a blog.

I have a soft spot for blogs. Many years ago, I became a dad blogger before it was cool to be a dad blogger — and I loved it. It also taught me something important: A blog is a place for you to share rich, relevant and useful information (more on this in the blog section of the book).

For starters, it's uncouth to use your blog as a place for a hard sell, so don't. Sure, what you write about can relate to what you do for a living, but it shouldn't be a sales pitch.

That said, you can use conversion in a handful of different ways on your blog:

1. Related Topics CTAs
    At the end of your blog, you can lead someone to other blog posts that have a similar topic to what they've just read. For instance, I wrote a series of articles that revolved around goals, one of which was titled Running a Small Business and the Art of Setting Goals. This series has multiple related articles, so I listed them at the bottom of the blog post:

    - Running a Small Business & the Art of Balance
    - Running a Small Business & the Art of Discovering Goals
    - Running a Small Business & the Art of Defining Goals
    - Running a Small Business & the Art of Overcoming Obstacles
    - Running a Small Business & the Art of Setting a Date on Your Goals

    As you can see, this is not a hard conversion; it's a soft one that revolves around the simple fact that if someone liked the article and read it to the end, that person might be interested in reading more about the subject. If so, let's make it easy (good UX)! And although we're not leading someone to a product or service page, clicking on one of the related blog posts keeps the reader on our site, further develops our digital relationship, and begins to build trust ... all good things.

2. Text Link and Button CTAs
    If a blog post relates to a product or service you offer, you could place a CTA at the end of the post. You can do this with a text link or a more traditional CTA button.

    a. **Text Link CTA.** In the blog post *The Rise of HTTPS*, we talk all about the growing importance of having a site that's HTTPS versus HTTP.

"As of October 2017, Google has rolled out some changes regarding HTTP and HTTPS on their Chrome web browser. This change has made it important for every business to consider switching their site over to HTTPS — because Google has informed us that HTTPS is now a ranking signal ..."

The article goes on to clarify and explain this statement, and it discusses the implications of what this Google change could mean (remember Mobilegeddon?).

The blog post wraps up by advising readers to talk with their web developer about making the change to HTTPS ASAP. This recommendation doesn't ask for anything; it instead delivers valuable advice for anyone who has a website.

But what if the reader isn't happy with a certain web developer? Or what if the reader has a self-created site and has no idea how to make it HTTPS?

Knowing this will be the case for some readers, we post the following text link at the end of the blog post:

"If you have questions or need help with the process, feel free to contact Cuppa SEO anytime."

The idea here is to offer help *without being pushy ...* no fear tactics, no arm twisting, just an offer to help. As you can see, this is not quite as soft a sell, but it is much softer than "you'd better call us now before your website blows up with hacks from Pluto!" (Did you know it was reclassified as a planet in 2017?).

b. **Button CTA.** Here's where things could get messy. An invisible line exists between a website's homepage and subpage strategy versus its blog strategy. And because it's invisible, it's easy to cross that line if you don't know it's there.

On a homepage or subpage, a CTA button is totally acceptable and often helpful to the visitor (as long as it follows the criteria we discussed earlier).

On a blog, this same type of CTA button can appear spammy, pushy and even damage trust, because it changes the blog post from relationship building to a transaction. There's a certain "ewww" factor when you do this on a blog. Unless you have a sound reason to add a CTA button to a blog post, avoid it.

What's a GOOD reason to have a CTA button in a blog post? To make it easy for someone to download a white paper, ebook or infographic (in other words, "if you liked the value we gave you in this blog post, here's more …"). In all these cases, we're still in giving mode, although we might be asking for someone's contact information, too, which makes it give and take. If this is the case, what you're giving had better be compelling and deliver lots of value.

CONVERSION IN YOUR SOCIAL MEDIA

In many ways, the goal of social media conversion is similar to website conversion — to have visitors take the next step you want them to take.

This next step can be to guide a visitor to a specific web page or blog post (that pays off the social media post), or it could be something different — buying a product on Facebook, for example, or following a company page on LinkedIn.

At Cuppa SEO, we mostly use social media to encourage (convert) people to read our blog, a step that helps build trust and offers relevant information to people who need it. Of course, it brings more visitors to my website, and if they like what they've read, they now can check out the rest of the site or read more blog posts.

That said, social media can also be used to convert someone to a product or service. There's nothing wrong with that; just be sure you're *offering value and solutions* on social media, making it all about the reader. What you offer won't be for everybody, but if you strike a chord with those who do need what you offer, there's a better chance they'll click on your call-to-action.

Let's take a quick look at how conversion works with imagery, text links and buttons within your social media efforts.

1. Imagery: Have you ever clicked an image on social media, expecting to be led to more info, only to be presented with a BIGGER version of the image? Me, too. And this is the worst conversion — not to mention UX payoff — you could ask for.

   Sometimes this simply can't be helped. But if your imagery is clickable AND leads to the content highlighted in your post, that's perfect! Here's an example from a LinkedIn post ...

The image you see is pulled directly by LinkedIn into this post. In other words, the image lives on our Web Design web page; LinkedIn sees it and automatically pulls it in. And if someone clicks on it, it takes them exactly where they expect to go (which, of course, is where we want them to go, too).

That said, it isn't always possible to do this, because sometimes an image looks great on your website but renders badly on social media. Or something looks great on social media but awful on your site. When this is the case, I typically defer to ensuring things look good on the site, and then I simply choose/create a different image for social media. When this is the case, you wind up with a LinkedIn image that doesn't link to anything. (I don't know why LinkedIn doesn't allow us to embed a destination link into imagery.)

The ins and outs of how to ensure that your image leads to the actual homepage, subpage or blog post you're highlighting is discussed in step-by-step detail later in the book when we talk about how to actually *apply* conversion into your social media. For now, just know that the image in your social media post is a powerful way to convert.

2. Text Links: In the same LinkedIn example, you'll find a text link at the end of the copy (above the picture). As with our photo, this text link leads directly to our Web Design page.

    If the viewer has interest in our web design services, we've given them TWO ways to visit our Web Design page for more info. Why does this matter? Because we can't predict the behavior of the folks who see our post. Some will click on the photo, some will click on the text link. Either way, we're meeting their expectations by leading them to where they expect to go, which is good for conversion and UX!

3. CTA Buttons: Some social media platforms allow you to include a button when you publish a post. On platforms such as Facebook, this is typically associated with paid services such as Boost Post. Google has toyed with allowing businesses to use buttons for free on their increasingly useful "Post" option in Google My Business.

    Here are options Facebook offers when you boost a post ...

Buttons won't be right for every situation or organization, but they will be awesome for some — if you are selling a product (for example a book) on Facebook.

As with everything we're discussing here, you've got to think it through to ensure that you're honoring the person who's viewing your post. And if a button makes you say, "ewww," it will probably make others say it, too (hey, that rhymes), which means you need to get rid of it!

Speaking of "ewww," let's take a look at what I like to call ...

THE DARK SIDE OF CONVERSION
In addition to being a really cool title, the dark side of conversion identifies questionable tactics such as having someone fill out a form for ONE ebook, and then harassing them, almost daily, with an overzealous email campaign. I don't know about you, but I don't want to be harassed by someone I never wanted in my inbox in the first place.

And although the conversion sections of the book focus primarily on strategies that revolve around calls-to-action, I felt this was too important to leave out. So, let's take a look at ...

The Dark Side of Conversion: Treating People Like Fish

After careful review of this title, you might be wondering ... how in the world could a business treat a person like a fish?

It's pretty simple, really.

When trying to gain new clients or customers, some businesses perceive their potential customers as fish. Or at least they seem to, because they take out their fishing rod and drop a hook in the water with some enticing "bait" on it. Of course, the fishing rod is metaphorical, but the process that transpires is very much like fishing. The bait is something that, at first glance, seems irresistible — and oftentimes a bit too good to be true.

For instance, I recently signed up for a free webinar to help me attract more participants to *my own* webinars. The Facebook ad for the event was liked by many of my friends and colleagues, and it promised to be a "master class" with "incredible value," offering solid strategies to help me pack the house. I figured it might be worth my time, even if I gleaned only one good bit of info.

Once I signed up, it was all downhill from there. Let's dissect what happened ...

1. I had signed up the night before the webinar. In less than 24 hours, I received FIVE emails from the facilitator of the webinar, each one trying to hype me up and add importance to the webinar I had already signed up for — and reinforcing that I simply must attend. This is just a bad user experience (UX). I signed up for a free event, and I wound up with a stalker girlfriend who simply wouldn't leave me alone for more than a few hours! We've all had this happen though, right? Sign up for some "free" information, only to find that we're now "buddies" with someone we didn't want to hear from in the first place. This is a HUGE mistake in the conversion process, but it's rampant.

2. When the webinar started, I noticed that it was pre-recorded, and the facilitator wasn't even on screen! The information, which was a slideshow with audio, was infantile and maybe had value for someone who knew nothing about webinars. There certainly wasn't any info on how to gain more attendees. So I left, figuring that was that.

3. Until I started receiving multiple follow-up emails. I kept unsubscribing, and eventually the emails stopped. Now, it's one thing to get in touch with people (who have given you permission to do so) once in a while. But you'd better offer something of real value and not just be harassing them.

At this point, I strongly suspected that I was the victim of being treated like a fish. The line was cast and the tasty bait taken. The thing is, many others who attended this webinar probably felt the same way I did. But organizations that "go fishing" like this don't care. They are trying to get as many people as possible caught on their hooks, and then they're on to the next round of fishing before you know it. Some of the people who come to the webinar will surely spend money, but most won't. With this type of model, that's expected. It's a volume thing, a numbers game, where the need to create meaningful relationships is replaced by the need to find paying fish.

To be sure, I checked the facilitator's website and found that what she was really trying to do was get us to sign up for her paid service, which is lifetime membership to her "Webinars that Convert" content ...

This is all part of a calculated conversion strategy, but it lives on the "dark side" of conversion, where potential customers are not treated like people. Instead, they're commoditized (like fish), and corralled into a funnel (ok, so fish aren't technically corralled, but you get the idea) to see how many of them are profitable.

As we've discussed, conversion is a strategy that takes a visitor from where they are to where you want them to go. Whether it's to download a free ebook, fill out a form, make a call or some similar action, we know the conversion process often begins by having someone click on a button or text link. In the case we're dissecting, the first CTA is to sign up for the free webinar. The second is to make a purchase. And although this isn't always a bad conversion strategy, it's missing one main ingredient — VALUE in the freebie.

Make sure you're ALWAYS DELIVERING VALUE in your freebie. Because when you do, you stop treating people like fish and ...

... *Start Teaching People How to Fish!*

A very different philosophy — teaching people how to fish — empowers them with relevant, helpful information right from the get-go, *without* asking them for anything in return. It's relationship-based, as opposed to the numbers game being played when you treat people like fish.

When you empower your clients, you're giving them some of the tools they need to take care of their business themselves — and treating them like human beings along the way. Or, quite often, you're simply educating them as to what they need (and what they don't need) so they have a clear understanding of where they should apply their budget.

And in doing so, you're building TRUST, which is essential for any long-term relationship. Working with the relationship-based model doesn't mean you're giving away the entire farm, so to speak, or making your business nonessential in the process. In fact, it can often make you *more* essential, because you will be perceived as the true expert who's not afraid to share knowledge.

For instance, at Cuppa SEO, we like to help clients, potential clients — and anybody else who will listen — learn how to brew a better blog. That's why we've created our *Blogging 101 Ebook* based on the philosophy of teaching people how to fish. If you sign up for the ebook, you won't be bombarded with daily or weekly emails. You might receive a friendly, information-packed **monthly** newsletter that contains things like popular blog posts, free webinars and our upcoming Facebook Live events. That's it ... maximum once a month. Nice, right?

Well, all this talk of fish has put me in the mood for a cup of coffee (weird, I know). Time to brew up a fresh pot before we continue talking about The Dark Side of Conversion.

The Dark Side of Conversion: Desperation

Conversion can be a tricky strategy.

When handled incorrectly, even the most helpful intentions might come off as desperate (I call it Hungry Wolf Syndrome).

Case in point: When shopping for a holiday gift for my wife, I wanted to see how much shipping would cost for the item in my cart. To learn that, I needed to enter some personal info — including my email address (really?).

It was all downhill from there ...

Shipping was almost as much as the item, so I decided to buy from Amazon at a far lower cost. When I checked my email, I was surprised to find ... (drumroll for first conversion faux pas) ... that I had somehow signed up for the company's newsletter!

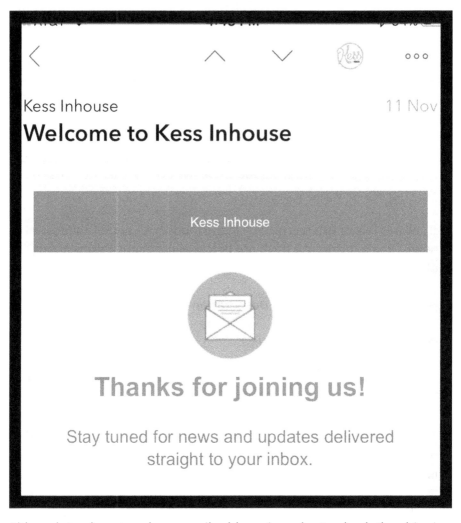

Although I only entered my email address in order to check the shipping cost (and potentially complete the order), they decided that was permission to place me on their email list.

Later that evening, I received the following email, which reminded me I had an unpurchased item in my cart.

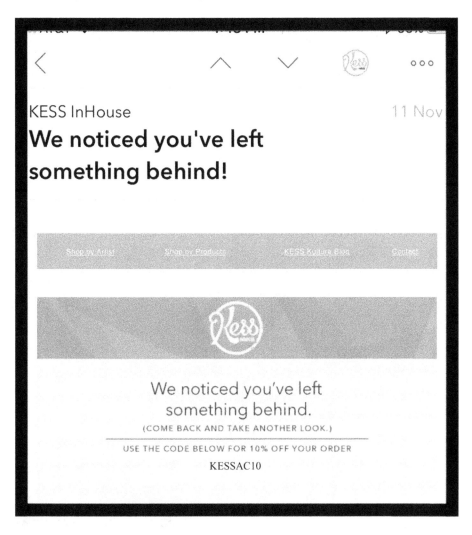

OK, one reminder might be a good thing. Maybe I had to get the kids to bed — or something — and just forgot to finish my order. But within just hours — at 3:15 a.m. — I received a SECOND reminder (faux pas #2).

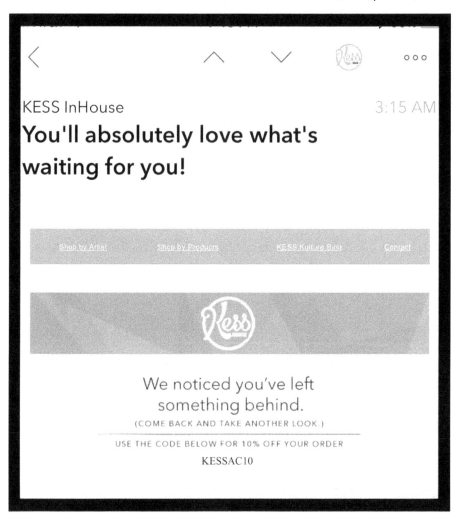

Now, this company is really starting to smell of desperation. Someone on the team decided — or was instructed by management — to pummel me with reminders to buy from them. This is an example of the Hungry Wolf Syndrome at its worst. I could almost see their marketing and sales department drooling for the sale, ribs protruding from hunger, eyes ablaze with the need to convert.

And then the wolf's howl came again at 7:50 a.m. — a third reminder within twelve hours (faux pas #3)!

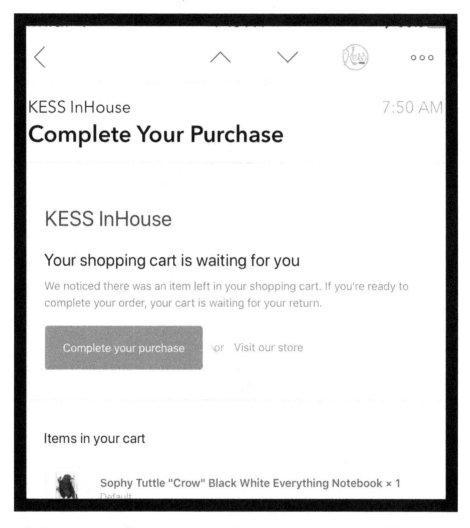

Whether it was well-meaning, sales driven, or just plain lack of knowledge about conversion, this company did a great job of turning me completely off.

The desperation was palpable.

When it comes to conversion of any kind, examine your process and your strategies to make sure you're adding value and developing relationships — as opposed to being perceived as a hungry wolf.

The Dark Side of Conversion: The Funny Thing About Sales Funnels

Remember when we mentioned "funnels" earlier? Well, it's time to swing back around to this concept for a closer look ...

The sales funnel is a tool that can drive the "buying process" from the first introduction to the purchase of a product or service.

The great thing about a sales funnel is that it's trackable, which means it can shed light on where the buying process may be breaking down. It's meant to track how many potential leads you get versus how many of them become actual customers.

Each step of the funnel can be adjusted to try to move more people from the top of the funnel to the bottom where they actually make a purchase.

Beyond this, the sales funnel concept has some major flaws ...

The Problem with Sales Funnels

Even though this is only a tool — a way of verbalizing a process of garnering business — it can easily have an effect on our thinking ... and how we treat people.

For starters, the term "sales funnel" objectifies a living, breathing person into a thing we must push through our funnel. It takes the humanity out of a customer and manifests in/as a process to increase revenue, as opposed to being a process to help others solve problems.

Again, I know this is only a way to verbalize a process, **but the words we use have power.**

And the perception that's created with a sales funnel is almost like transforming a person into an object — like a pinball — that needs to be pushed to a particular place to produce a sale.

When you look at each person you meet as a potential "sale," you feed the sales funnel. The problem: NOBODY likes to be sold.

The Relationship Funnel
Instead, let's get rid of the word altogether and create a "Relationship Funnel." Instead of trying to drive a person down to a sale, we work on developing relationships — one person at a time.

These relationships will inevitably fall into a handful of categories:
1. People who become friends or colleagues
2. People whom we learn from or who learn from us
3. People who become clients or customers
4. People you don't ever want to talk to — ever again, for whatever reason

The people who become customers don't become customers because we've "sold" them. They become customers because through relationship development, we've learned what their problems are, and they've learned that we can help find solutions.

Consider the classic networking event as an example.

Let's say you attend a networking event with a goal of finding three "hot leads" — good candidates as sales prospects. This sales-funnel mentality objectifies others; it's superficial and egotistical. It makes it all about *you* and growing your business.

It's another form of Hungry Wolf Syndrome. The wolf stalks the room looking for a meal ... er, I mean a sale.

With the relationship funnel, you enter that same room with a very different mindset. You're taking every interaction as an opportunity to develop a relationship and see where it goes. And *if* you meet people who appear to be a good fit to become your customer, your job is to see if you can help solve their problems and pain points, not push them through a funnel so you can get paid.

Instead of asking ourselves how many hot leads we're going to get, we're asking ourselves "What relationships will I develop today?"

Don't get me wrong: Many businesses truly want to add value for each customer and to be of help. But when we use words that imply a different directive, it drives our actions in a different way.

In the words of Muhammad Ali, "What you are thinking about is what you are becoming." I don't know about you, but I don't want to be a guy who sells stuff and pushes people into a funnel. That's no fun. I prefer to look at each interaction as an opportunity to build a relationship. I've seen firsthand how this philosophy can help you build a successful business while being perceived as an authentic professional. And with the content marketing philosophy solidly in place — both online and in the physical world — the more we align ourselves with relationship-building and shed the old sales funnel philosophy, the better off we'll be.

The Dark Side of Conversion: A List of Strategies to Avoid

Because I don't want to spend too much time on the "dark side," I'm going to finish off this section with a bulleted list of no-no's ...

- Spamming people with emails after they've opted-in
- Adding people to your email list WITHOUT their permission (Just because they gave you their business card doesn't mean they've opted into your newsletter or offers)
- Videos that pretend you are my friend (You're not my buddy!)
- Videos that bait instead of educate
- Over-promising, under-delivering, and then charging for the "actual insights"
- Slick, slimy used-car-salesman syndrome: When you see it enough times, you might think this is the "right way" to do a call-to-action/

video (Remember: Everyone put asbestos in walls until it became obvious that it was unhealthy). Doing something because you see it elsewhere is NOT a good reason. Doing it because you think it's effective, or because you or your team respond well to it IS a good reason to try it — so TEST IT and see if your visitors like it, too.

- Avoid manipulation: Don't follow this well-known conversion expert's sickening advice ...

   "We do not want to start sending traffic to our website until we have a well-oiled mouse trap with fresh cheese set." — Chris Smith

   If you start looking at your visitors and potential customers this way, you've lost the whole point of online marketing — which is to develop relationships, not to deceive or twist someone's arm to buy.

- Too many CTAs on a page:
   - They're bad for conversion
   - They're bad for UX
   - In this example, there are 14 tabs in the navigation, at least 12 CTAs above the navigation, and a minimum of 8 CTAs on the page — and that's before you scroll. That equals 34 items for a visitor to digest on the homepage. This is a conversion and UX nightmare ...

PART 2: YOUR WEBSITE

Now that we've gained a solid understanding of what search engine optimization (SEO), user experience (UX) and conversion (CV) are, let's dive into how you can apply these strategies into your website.

As discussed, your online marketing efforts are components of a larger unit, a bit like how hundreds of car parts come together to make one automobile. When constructed correctly, *in the right order*, your car will move, keep you safe and get you to your destination.

From the engine, to the wheels, to the AC — and of course the coffee-cup holder — all of these parts work as one cohesive unit.

The same is true of online marketing. Projects and tasks need to be completed in a certain order and in a certain way. Otherwise, you wind up with a lot of parts that aren't working well together, which often results in wasted time and money.

So where do we begin? What's the starting point on the road to successful holistic online marketing?

IT ALL BEGINS WITH YOUR WEBSITE
Your website is the foundation of your online marketing efforts. It's the place where people come to learn more about your company, buy a product or service, or find out how to get in touch with you.

Your website comes first because it's literally the hub in the wheel of your efforts.

For example:
- Your blog needs a place to live where it can inform and build trust. When your blog is built into your website, it's easy for customers to check out the rest of your site.

- You can't implement SEO into a website that doesn't exist! So SEO can't come before your website, although it can be developed *while* your site is being built.
- You need a website on which to build good user experience (UX) and conversion (CV) strategies.

Although these points all seem obvious, you'd be surprised how many clients come to us feeling as though they have to get started with social media or blogging when it's their website that needs attention first.

Chapters in this part of the book will dive into the following topics:

Chapter 4: Making Your Website "Customer Facing"
In other words, make it about your customers and potential customers — not about you. It's tempting to talk about the "25 years of experience" your company has, or highlight your awards. Frankly speaking, nobody really cares. Customers want to know if you can address their pain points.

To help make your website as customer facing as possible, we'll also focus on:
- Whether or not your content is rich and relevant — and why this is important
- Three "magic" questions you can ask about every piece of content your write to ensure that it's as benefit-driven as possible! You'll quickly find that these questions are something to keep in mind throughout all aspects of your online marketing.

Chapter 5: Search Engine Optimization (SEO)
In Part 1, you gained a clear understanding of SEO. Now, it's time to take a look at how to *apply* SEO into your website.

We'll be focusing specifically on *how to*:
- Create a killer keyword report
- Implement keywords into all areas of your website

This chapter also goes beyond the implementation process to focus on:
- Showing you how to ensure your website is mobile friendly
- Top 10 Google Panda do's and don'ts
- Backlinks and citations

- Improving your website's page load time
- Optimizing image file size
- The importance of HTTPS

Chapter 6: User Experience (UX)

In this chapter, we'll be performing what I like to refer to as a website assessment — or in this case, examining a handful of websites that provide an outstanding UX.

It's a heuristic approach to analyzing and optimizing the user experience on your website, offering hands-on learnings on how to apply a great UX to your own site.

Specifically, you'll learn how to:
- Assess the user experience of every page of your website, for desktop and mobile, respectively
- Review the hierarchy of each page, including: navigation (architecture), homepage and subpage layout (aesthetic), as well as optimal placement of elements like images, copy, and calls-to action (CTAs).

Chapter 7: Conversion (CV)

Now that we've got visitors feeling good about where they've arrived (thanks to our most excellent user experience), we need a solid conversion strategy to ensure they know exactly what to do next.

In this chapter, we'll look at how to apply your learnings about CV from Part 1 of this book into your website. Specifically, we'll focus on:
- Website conversion on your homepage
- Web design and the art of conversion
- Website conversion on your subpages
- The lifecycle of a call-to-action
- Why carousels, parallax websites and pop-ups should be avoided

4. Making Your Website "Customer Facing"

In other words, make it about your customers and potential customers — not about you.

In working with hundreds of clients, I've found that many of them struggle with similar issues. In fact, hearing the same pain points over and over was the inspiration for the Holistic Guide to Online Marketing workshop, which eventually became this book.

I mention this here because I want you to know that *many organizations* believe they need to share their accolades and experience to clients and potential clients — right on their website's homepage. Sometimes this sharing occurs because there's a belief that awards are impressive and might be the tipping point in gaining more business. Sometimes an organization wants to share simply because there's a rich company history they want everyone to know about — whether it's being in business for over a century, or being completely employee owned, there's an authentic excitement about the organization that management and team members want to share.

Frankly speaking, nobody really cares.

At least not when they first arrive on your website. When they first arrive on your site's homepage, a visitor wants to know — often times, right away — if you can fix their problem, and ease their pain. This isn't to say that your company's awards and heritage aren't important, they just typically shouldn't be taking up prime real estate on your homepage. Instead, use that space for benefit-driven, customer-centric content.

Think about it. Let's say you're looking for a local yoga studio. You need to lower your stress, get in some physical activity — and nurture your spirit with a meditative practice.

You're also exhausted, work full-time and have two kids, which means you want a good solution as fast and easy as possible.

You do a local search, which in my neck of the woods might look like: "Yoga Studio Madison WI," which leads you to one of Cuppa SEO's customers, EarthView Yoga.

Now, the owners of EarthView have some pretty impressive credentials. But as you can see, we're not presented with them. Instead, we're given a very customer-centric headline, "Discover freedom in your mind, body and breath. Discover EarthView Yoga. Discover Yourself."

This is followed by two calls-to-action, which I refer to as *the first date vs. the introduction*. Although we'll be discussing this concept later in the book, it's important to mention here because these calls-to-action are both customer-centric.

Schedule a Class (the first date) leads visitors right to a page where they can schedule a class (if they're ready to do so). Learn More About Us (the introduction) is for those who aren't ready to take the plunge into a "first date" and need to learn more about what they can expect from EarthView to see if it's right for them.

Below the intentionally simple headline "Welcome to EarthView Yoga," you'll find more benefit-driven, customer-focused content ...

Welcome to EarthView Yoga
An oasis for self-care and healing in the heart of Madison.

As soon as you enter our warm, spacious yoga studio you'll begin to feel more grounded, centered and relaxed. EarthView provides a beautiful environment to cultivate the strength, balance, flexibility and mental clarity achieved through a committed yoga practice.

Yoga classes for all levels

We offer a broad range of classes for all levels — from beginner to experienced yogi — taught by some of the finest teachers in the Midwest. Through a technique called creative sequencing, our teachers can help you improve your strength and flexibility, no matter what your fitness level. This results in significant stress relief and a heightened level of freedom from fatigue — and who doesn't need that?

What to expect at EarthView

EarthView combines all the elements of a great yoga studio into one package.

- Incredible teachers who are dedicated to your fitness, health and wellbeing
- Personalized attention that helps you advance as a student
- A beautiful, spacious yoga studio with an eco-friendly bamboo floor, and floor-to-ceiling windows
- Professional-grade sound and lighting system that adds to the overall experience
- Clean, spacious and comfortable bathrooms — with showers!
- Friendly, helpful desk staff, and a welcoming lobby that's designed to help you relax
- Complimentary tea for connection before and after class (we love our tea!)
- Complimentary mats (if you need one) and a mountain of props to support your practice

Ready to give EarthView a try?

Visit our Class Packages and Memberships page to sign up for a single drop-in class, one-month of unlimited yoga classes (for new students) — and many more options here at our studio.

Thank you for visiting EarthView Yoga. We hope to see you soon!

In case your eyes are like mine, and it's hard to read the screen shot, here is the content in bigger print ...

Welcome to EarthView Yoga
An oasis for self-care and healing in the heart of Madison.

As soon as you enter our warm, spacious yoga studio you'll begin to feel more grounded, centered and relaxed. EarthView provides a beautiful environment to cultivate the strength, balance, flexibility and mental clarity achieved through a committed yoga practice.

Yoga classes for all levels
We offer a broad range of classes for all levels — from beginner

to experienced yogi — taught by some of the finest teachers in the Midwest. Through a technique called creative sequencing, our teachers can help you improve your strength and flexibility, no matter what your fitness level. This results in significant stress relief and a heightened level of freedom from fatigue — and who doesn't need that?

What to expect at EarthView
EarthView combines all the elements of a great yoga studio into one package:

- Incredible teachers who are dedicated to your fitness, health and wellbeing
- Personalized attention that helps you advance as a student
- A beautiful, spacious yoga studio with an eco-friendly bamboo floor, and floor-to-ceiling windows
- Professional-grade sound and lighting system that adds to the overall experience
- Clean, spacious and comfortable bathrooms — with showers!
- Friendly, helpful desk staff, and a welcoming lobby that's designed to help you relax
- Complimentary tea for connection before and after class (we love our tea!)
- Complimentary mats (if you need one) and a mountain of props to support your practice

Ready to give EarthView a try?
Visit our Class Packages and Memberships page to sign up for a single drop-in class, one-month of unlimited yoga classes (for new students) — and many more options here at our studio.

Thank you for visiting EarthView Yoga. We hope to see you soon!

Now imagine how you'd feel if this homepage told a different story: one where the calls-to-action were removed, and instead of being benefit-driven, the content below the headline were all about the owners' experience ... where they've studied, how long they've been in business, what they ate for dinner last night. Just kidding on that last part, but you get the point — this version is all about THEM, not the visitor! It would have nothing to do with solving the visitor's needs.

Of course, we're talking in extremes here, but I want you to get a clear idea of what it means to make your website more about your visitors and less about you. Which brings us to the question ...

IS YOUR CONTENT RICH AND RELEVANT — OR JUST PLAIN YUCKY?
As discussed, copy (also referred to as content) that lives on your website and blog needs to be rich, relevant and benefit-driven. It has to solve problems — and maybe even identify problems your customers didn't know they had.

If your content talks about benefits and value, it's not only helpful to visitors, it's also a great start on the path to solid SEO.

You might be asking, "How the heck do I accomplish this rich content thing, Joey"?

Three "Magic" Questions to Ask for Every Web Page
Well, to ensure your copy packs the most value possible, always do your best to CLEARLY and SUCCINCTLY answer these three "magic" questions on every web page:
1.   What is it?
2.   What does it do?
3.   How does it help me (benefits)?

I call them magic questions because they get to the heart of what your content needs to contain.

Google likes relevant content, and just like the human eye, it's judging your content to determine if it's rich and relevant, or boring, "thin" and yucky.

Rich content helps each of your web pages and blog posts gain more authority in Google's eyes, which means better ranking in search results.

Thin content accomplishes the opposite and may lead your website or blog toward what I call the "black hole of Google Panda" — never to be found in organic search results.

The good news is that if you're taking the time to avoid the yuck factor and create quality content, you site is already partially optimized!

Why It's Important
This is an important consideration to keep in mind no matter what part of your website you're working on. Whether it's SEO, UX or conversion, the more you're able to make your efforts customer-centric and benefit-driven (addressing those pain points), the better chance you have of building a relationship with each visitor.

This relationship-building philosophy also holds true with your blog and social media campaigns, but more on those in Part 3 and Part 4, respectively.

In essence, when you make your website customer centric, it can naturally help improve the overall user experience of your site. It can also improve your conversion rate, because you've clearly defined how you can help.

5. Search Engine Optimization (SEO)

THE KEYWORD REPORT

Before we begin optimizing a website, the first thing we do at Cuppa SEO is thoroughly research and test a very long list of keywords and keyword phrases. It's how we identify which keywords are optimal for a client's website.

Many factors go into deciding if a keyword is right for a particular client. Some of them are researched through online tools, and others are examined in a more "analog" way — through the filter of my own eyes and brain. After optimizing thousands of pages, I've learned that there are very subtle factors that go into proper keyword selection — much too subtle for an algorithm or app to identify. Luckily, thanks to the fact that my brain is typically caffeinated with a hot cup of coffee, I'm able to discern these factors that ultimately help our clients' websites rank higher in natural search results.

Creating a keyword report before optimizing a website is incredibly important. Some web developers claim they know SEO, but they have only a basic understanding of the art of optimization. The result can be a keyword report (if one is even produced) that is often superficial, inaccurate and incomplete.

Your keyword report is critical; it should be your touchstone for SEO implementation into your website, blog and social media, so it has to be done right. Here's a list of questions to consider as well as some guidance on how to create a killer keyword report that's accurate, thorough and customized for your business.

Put on a pot of coffee, and let's get started.

Holistic Side Note: Although we're talking about your website here, you may see an occasional shout out to blogs. Why? Because a blog is typically part of a website, and has a direct impact on the SEO of the site as a whole. Now, back to our scheduled programming ...

8 Questions (and Answers) to Get You Started

1) *How do I choose my initial list of keywords?*
   To begin, you'll need to create a list of "common sense keywords." Make a list of keywords you think (or know) people use when searching for what you do. To compile the list, you can also ask team members, colleagues and customers what keyword phrases they would use to find/describe someone who does what you do.

   Next, review the content on your website (if you have one), as well as the content on your top 3–4 competitors' websites. Add to your list of common-sense keywords anything that looks like it might be a good keyword phrase. While you're working on this, you might come up with keyword iterations on your own. Add them to the list.

Holistic Side Note: When I perform this initial research for a keyword report, I often find that my client's competition is marginally optimized at best. It makes for a good start, because it gives us a better chance to crush them in natural search rankings — in the nicest way possible, of course. Following the step-by-step guidelines in this chapter can help you do the same.

   Once you're done putting together your initial keyword list, it's time for research ...

2) *What's the best way to perform keyword research?*
   Include an accurate keyword tool that has the ability to provide results by specific region — city, state and country. At the writing of this book, my favorite keyword tool that provides this regional

search is: KWFinder.com. There are others out there, but KWFinder is my preferred SEO tool because it offers a faster search function, coupled with more relevant information at my fingertips.

If you're a national company, city and state becomes less important. A national company can consider using two additional keyword planners: MOZ Keyword Explorer and SEMrush. Again, these are effective only if you're a national organization that's NOT looking to focus on any region(s) at a city or state level. All three of the recommendations included here are paid services, but they are well worth the investment as long as you USE the tool.

As mentioned earlier, you'll also need to implement keyword relevance testing that's performed the old-fashioned way — with one's eyes and brain. Although this takes time, practice and patience, questions 2 through 8 will help you along your way.

3) *What's a good number of monthly searches for a keyword phrase?*
The short answer is, it depends (sorry, I know that's not what you wanted to hear). Many factors come into play when benchmarking the minimal number of monthly searches a keyword phrase needs to be relevant for your website — like the region(s) where your company does business, website age, website size, overall website authority and market competition, among other factors. Just remember, a higher number of monthly searches isn't always better. Instead, you want to find the best keywords out there for your particular circumstances. This brings us to our next question ...

4) *What kind of competition level are you using as your benchmark?*
The answer here is similar to the answer to question #3: It depends. And while lower competition is always what we're striving for, there are instances where a website will compete just fine (or even dominate) against high competition.

For example, a company like Home Depot can use any keyword phrase it wants. They're a "big fish," no matter what body of water they're swimming in — even if it's the Pacific Ocean (which happens to be the largest ocean in the world)! On the other hand, the corner hardware store doesn't have a chance to compete on Home Depot's level, which means it shouldn't try to use the same high-competition keywords. Instead, the local store should put together a keyword report that includes keyword phrases they're going to be able to rank well for. These phrases will most likely have lower monthly search volume, but they'll also have less competition.

Search-to-Competition Ratio

Here's a big-picture answer to questions #2 and #3: At the end of the day, you want to rank well for the keywords you choose to implement into your website and blog. To do this, you've got to find the right "search-to-competition ratio" for your particular business.

In other words, if you're a local (regional) business, and you've got a good possibility of ranking well for a set of keyword phrases that get only 20–30 hits each per month, that's a lot better on average than implementing keywords that get hundreds or thousands of hits per month that you're never going to rank well for.

Think of it like a tennis match. You might be good enough to dominate in local amateur tournaments, but you'd be hard pressed to even score a point against top players like Nadal or Federer. Stay within the competition pool you can dominate. You'll gain traction online and actually get more visitors to your website.

5) *How do you test keyword phrases for relevance?*
The most dependable method is typically manually, one phrase at a time. You literally have to go to Google and enter the term you are researching. Is it relevant to the products or services you offer? Or is it not what you thought?

Consider the example of "digital asset management," also known as DAM, an acronym that is understood within the industry. A quick Google search reveals that this acronym has no SEO value for digital asset management because it produces search results about actual dams that control water. It's not a keyword that any digital asset management company should use — ever.

In addition, sometimes a keyword will be good for a products or services page, while other times it might be good only for a blog post. You would not know unless you were testing your keyword phrases in natural Google search results.

For example, when I search "Ice Cream," Google delivers results that include local ice cream shops, which of course is a product-based result. Google delivers this type of result because it believes (rightly so, thanks to its human-like algorithm) that when someone searches for "Ice Cream," that person wants to go to an ice cream shop and eat it (I'll bet this is not the last of my food analogies). We can deduce that the keyword phrase "Ice Cream" is good to use if you sell ice cream.

Now, if I search "How to Make Ice Cream," my search results are all blogs and recipes on how to make ice cream. In this case, Google is telling me that when a person searches with this particular keyword phrase, they're looking for INFORMATION about how to make ice cream — not where to go to buy it — making "How to Make Ice Cream" a potentially great keyword phrase for a blog post, but a TERRIBLE keyword phrase for a products or services page.

Although this is an extreme example, it shows that it's not always obvious whether a keyword phrase is going to be good for products/services or for a blog post (or sometimes both), which is why each phrase has to be checked with your own eyes.

Yet it is an important differentiation because we (and Google) want visitors to be connected to exactly what they're expecting to find when they arrive on our website or blog. If they're expecting information on how to make ice cream, and we're trying to sell them a product or service, there's a disconnect — which will very likely result in the visitor hitting the back button to find a more relevant result.

6) *How do you determine which keywords to avoid?*
As you can see, sometimes there are keyword phrases that just

aren't relevant for one or more reasons. If that's the case, avoid them if you can, even if they have high search volume. Don't be lured into using a keyword phrase just because it has high search volume and low competition. If it's not relevant to what you do, you might get more traffic, but you certainly won't attain more business from this kind of practice.

That said, if you can't avoid using this type of keyword phrase because it occurs naturally in your content — maybe it's a product or service name — go ahead and use it (sparingly). Just don't treat it like a keyword or expect it to garner relevant traffic.

7) *What's about optimizing a website or blog based on region?*
Thanks to Google's ability to provide relevant regionalized search results, optimizing a local business by the region(s) where you do business is very important. Taking this into consideration while you're creating your keyword report helps ensure that your website will be optimized to compete with your local competitors, which is what you want.

To get started, if you're a local business begin adding your city and state to keywords you research. For example, if your keyword is "Dentist," try "Dentist San Francisco," and "Dentist San Francisco CA." If you're using the KWFinder application, it will give you iterations of these phrases, making it easier to identify additional regionalized keyword phrases.

8) *What does a keyword report look like?*
Here's a quick look at a sample Cuppa SEO Keyword Report. It gives you a good idea of what a completed report should look like so you can use it over and over — like a playbook — to help in all your online marketing efforts.

Cuppa SEO Keyword Reports are organized in a "good, better, best" format, so there's never any doubt as to which keywords are best to use ...

Cuppa SEO
Keyword Report for Cuppa SEO — September 15, 2015

Keyword Research
Research was performed for searches made throughout Dane County & USA. All numbers are based on monthly search totals.

Competition
List of competitors' websites, or companies that we aspire to be like.

BEST KEYWORDS

Keywords	Minn	Iowa	Competition
Sample Keyword 1	320	10	Low/--
Sample Keyword 2	1,000	480	Med/Low
Sample Keyword 3	1,000	390	Med/Low
Sample Keyword 4	480	110	Low/Low
Sample Keyword 5	90	40	Low/Low
Sample Keyword 6	590	260	Med/Med

GOOD KEYWORDS

Keywords	Minn	Iowa	Competition
Sample Keyword 7	480	210	High/Med
Sample Keyword 8	90	30	High/Medium
Sample Keyword 9	110	50	High/High
Sample Keyword 10	390	210	High/High
Sample Keyword 11	30	10	Med/Med
Sample Keyword 12	480	170	High/High

In this report, the keywords are on the left, followed by the number of MONTHLY searches for that keyword phrase by region (in this case, Minnesota and Iowa). For example, "Sample Keyword 1" has a search volume of 320 searches per month in Minnesota, and a search volume of 10 searches per month in Iowa.

To the far right, we see the Competition level that exists for each keyword, again by region. For "Sample Keyword 1" the competition is **Low** in Minnesota, and the -- means competition is virtually nonexistent in Iowa. When we create a report, we always identify competition as Low, Medium or High, based on the data we find in the keyword tool we're using (like KWFinder) — so at a glance we can get an accurate assessment of how stiff the competition is for any of our keywords.

How to Gain an SEO Advantage
At best, individuals who don't fully understand SEO typically choose keywords they believe people are searching for. At worst, they don't

purposefully choose any keywords at all. This puts them at a disadvantage versus a business that has taken the time or hired a professional to create a keyword report and implement optimal keywords into their website.

To gain an advantage over your competitors, you'll need to make sure you're using the very best keywords on each of your web pages in all of the key areas, which we'll be talking about next. Remember, these aren't always the keywords that get the most hits per month. Instead, they're the ones that are going to have the most impact on getting *you* found.

WHERE TO IMPLEMENT YOUR KEYWORDS
As you can see, the quality of your keywords makes a big difference in how effective they are, and a lot of factors go into determining which ones are best for your particular website and blog.

Once you've created a killer keyword report, the next natural question is, "Where do I use these keywords?"

When implementing SEO, it's important to affect every possible nook and cranny. Through the process of layering keywords into multiple areas, we create pages that are palatable to search engines yet natural-looking to the human eye.

Keywords and keyword phrases need to be implemented into:
1. Title Tags
2. Primary Headlines
3. Secondary Headlines
4. Image & Alternate Image Text
5. Content
6. Descriptive Links

1. Title Tags

These are the words (content) in the gray bar at the very top of each web page. Best practices dictate these should not exceed 70 characters, including spaces. Separate the phrases with "sticks" (not commas, periods or dashes), like this ...

2 & 3. Headlines

Implementing relevant keywords into each headline can help clarify page content and increase website authority with search engines.

This includes all types of headlines, but the three most widely used are:

- H1 Headline: This is the primary headline on a page, as shown in #2 above.
- H2 Headline: This is the secondary headline that can appear on a page.
- H3 Headlines: These are the smaller, third-tier headlines that can appear on a page as shown in #3 above.

Keep in mind that a web page or blog post should only have one H1 and one H2 headline. More than one H1 or H2 adds ambiguity, leaving Google questioning what's most important on the page, so avoid this mistake. If you want to use multiple headlines to help segment content, which I highly recommend, stick with H3s.

4. Image & Alternate Image Text (also referred to as Alt Text)

Although this is an important step in the optimization process, it's often overlooked. Optimizing both your image names and your alt image text helps Google identify what your imagery and graphics are about. Optimized images help improve the SEO value of your website and blog. They also make it possible for people to find you through the Google Images tab during an organic search. In the example below, I did a search for "SEO Madison WI." Note how the entire first row of search results in the Google Images tab are Cuppa SEO homepage images ...

Image Names
"Logo.png" or "Image12867.jpg" are meaningless to Google, so the algorithm just moves on and pays these images no mind. Instead, use a phrase that's rich in one or more keywords that are relevant to each particular page or blog post.

In other words, name that image. It will improve your SEO!

How to Implement an Optimized Image Name
1. It's best to optimize an image name BEFORE you upload it to your website or blog. But if you're beginning work on optimizing an existing website or blog, you won't have that luxury. If this is the case, you'll have to save your current website images to your computer or a cloud account like Dropbox or Box. Now you're ready to caffeinate each image with some SEO.

2. Take out your keyword report. It's the foundation for optimizing every image.
3. Assess what your image is about. For this example, let's say you own a dental office and you're optimizing an image for your root canal page.
4. The original image name is: "IMG_28651.jpg," which has neither SEO value nor value to the human eye.
5. You look at your keyword report and determine "Root Canal Madison WI" is a good keyword phrase for this image.
6. So you change the image name to "Root-Canal-Madison-WI.jpeg." Or even better, maybe you include your business name: "Caffeinated-Dentist-Root-Canal-Madison-WI.jpeg" (fictitious, of course).
7. Notice how I've structured the hierarchy of these image names with each word being separated by a dash. There are NO spaces, and NO underscores — both of which would hurt the SEO value of the image.
8. Now, within this one image name, "Caffeinated-Dentist-Root-Canal-Madison-WI.jpeg," I am actually using ALL of the following keywords:
   - Dentist
   - Dentist Madison
   - Dentist Madison WI
   - Root Canal
   - Root Canal Madison
   - Root Canal Madison WI

As you might have guessed, at first it may be a challenge for you to fit six different keyword phrases into one image name. It's not something I'm expecting you to be able to do out of the gate, but it's a good goal to shoot for as you become more and more comfortable with naming images.

Holistic Side Note: I actually used only two main keyword phrases here: 1. Dentist Madison WI; 2. Root Canal Madison WI. The other four keyword phrases are derivatives of these. I mention this because using six DIFFERENT keyword phrases would be way too much for a single image name.

Which brings us to ...

The do's & don'ts of image naming ...

When it comes down to choosing an image name, there are a few factors to consider:

1. Don't stuff them with keywords. In other words, make sure you're not creating image names that are 70+ characters long. In fact, even 60 characters can start reading like a stuffed turkey.

2. Instead keep image name length, whenever possible, to 50 or fewer characters — including hyphens between words. Although there's no hard rule that 50 is the magic number, optimizing thousands of images has made it clear to me that beyond 50 characters starts to look like stuffing. And if it appears that you are jamming in too many keywords, Google may take notice. If it does, your goal of adding SEO value to a page to increase its authority might backfire, with Google slapping you down and penalizing you for using what they consider to be "black hat" tactics.

3. Name logos, social media buttons and any other recurring images with more general keyword phrases, as they will be appearing on multiple pages.

4. Always use hyphens instead of underscores or spaces in image names.

5. Never use an "&" in your image name. Either spell out the word "and" or simply remove it. This rule can often come into play because it's totally OK to use an "&" in your alternate image text (alt text) — as you'll soon see — but you've got to remember to remove it or change it to an "and" in your image name. For the sake of saving space ("and" is three characters), I recommend just removing "and" from your image name, as long as it still makes sense.

Alternate Image Text (Alt Text)
Just as with your image name, it's important to name your alternate image text for SEO value. Let's talk about how this works.

Once you've named your image, the next step is to upload it to your website. When you do, you should be presented with the opportunity to add alternate image text to the image.

Here's an example of what this might look like when implementing an image into a Wordpress site ...

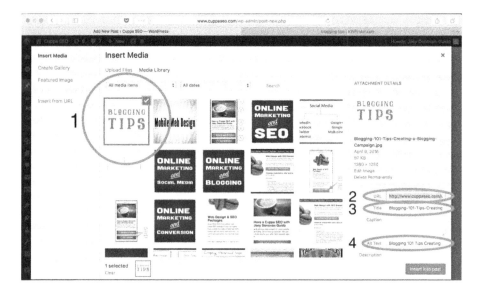

Here's what the image upload screen looks like in Wordpress (at the time of writing):

1. On the left, you'll see the actual image that I'm uploading.
2. On the right, you'll see that Wordpress has taken my image and created a URL for it. This is normal Wordpress functionality, and it's automatic so you don't have to worry about it. I'm only showing it to you here so you're not left scratching your head wondering about it.
3. The "Title" is actually the optimized name I gave my image. In this case, it's "Blogging-101-Tips-Creating-a-Blogging-Campaign" (BTW, titles have no SEO value)
4. To create the Alt Text, simply cut and paste the Title into the Alt Text field. Now, you've got to remove all hyphens and replace them with spaces. It's also nice to make sure each word is initial capped, too. Like this: "Blogging 101 Tips Creating a Blogging Campaign"

Why this is important

This is another area Google looks to in order to glean information when it's crawling a page. Originally intended to assist people with disabilities, Google also looks to alternate image text for SEO value and page clarification. Your alt text can typically repeat the image name you've chosen, but be sure to write it out just as you would a sentence as we did in the above example. Remember if you need an "&" in the alt image text, that's OK, just avoid them in image names.

In case you're wondering, this image was optimized for the following keyword phrases:
- Blogging
- Blogging 101
- Blogging Tips

This is a nice example of how layering keyword phrases works. Although I used just one phrase in the image and alt image name — "Blogging 101 Tips" — this single phrase contains three usable keywords/keyword phrases.

The do's & don'ts of alt image text naming ...
- Be sure to add optimized alternate image text to *every* image, as it improves SEO value.
- Keep length to approximately 50 characters or less, including spaces.
- Make sure your alt text reads more like a sentence (remove hyphens).
- You don't need to worry about optimizing the "title attribute" of an image, as it has no SEO value.

The stock photo dilemma
Who knew there was so much to talk about regarding proper image naming?

This final note isn't directly about image naming. But because we're talking about naming images, it's a good opportunity to talk about image quality.

And although a well-optimized stock photo won't hold any less SEO value with Google, there's a chance it may hold less value to the human eye — especially if it's a *generic stock photo*.

Cheap and easy to locate, generic stock photos are a temptation that must be resisted because they're also obvious to most savvy online visitors. And once someone spots a generic photo, there's a higher probability your entire brand may be perceived as generic.

The solution? Use of interesting, original imagery and graphics is always recommended. But there may be times — due to subject matter, budget or an impending deadline — that you have to use stock photos. If this is the case, our advice is to avoid generic stock photos. Take time to find stock images that are truly engaging, relevant and unique.

5. Content

In addition to writing great content, you'll also need to use primary, secondary and semantic keywords (discussed in Part 1, soon to be discussed further) in each web page or blog post. Use these in an organic way where they make sense throughout the copy. Be aware that there is no magic number of times a keyword needs to appear for Google to recognize it as an intentional keyword phrase. Instead, Google is looking for context usage and how it applies to all of the words on a particular page.

Stuffing

That being said, overuse of a keyword phrase is something to avoid at all costs. This is referred to as "stuffing," and although it's great on Thanksgiving, it's best to avoid stuffing altogether on your website and blog. Why? Because if you get caught stuffing keywords into your pages, you could get a serious penalty from Google, which can land you in what I call "the black hole of Google Panda."

In a nutshell, Panda is the algorithm Google uses to assess the website authority and SEO value of each page of your website, and your website as a whole. Best to stay on Panda's good side and avoid the black hole — so don't stuff!

Check out the following 1-minute video about stuffing — starring my kids — at: www.cuppaseo.com/cuppa-seo-blog. Search for "Stuffing" to watch the video.

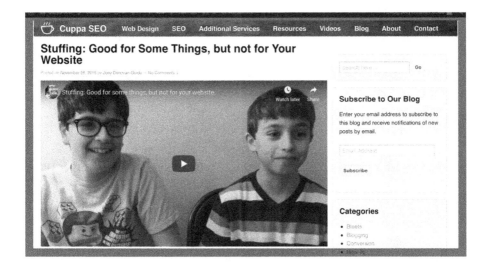

In a nutshell, keyword stuffing is exactly what it sounds like — jamming the same keyword or keyword phrase into your content as often as possible, just like the example Joss and Max provide in their video.

Reasons to avoid keyword stuffing are:

1) It has the potential to land you in the black hole of Google Panda. In non-tech terms, this means the page you stuff — and possibly your entire website — may never be found again in search engine results. Stuffing is bad for SEO, and just as importantly ...

2) Even if Google doesn't hit you with a heavy penalty, your readers will not appreciate this tactic, and they very likely won't come back. In other words, it's a bad user experience. There's a good chance you've seen writing like this on somebody's website: *"Our **dentist** will take very good care of you. Our **dentist** is a pain-free **dentist**, so make an appointment with the **dentist** today!"*

Yuck.

Now imagine this, paragraph after paragraph, page after page, and you can see why Google would place a site like this where the sun don't shine. = ^ O

There was a time, back in the wild west of the internet, where adding a bunch of the same keywords could elevate a page in search engine results. Google quickly said "no way!" to this tactic, labeling it black hat SEO for good reason.

As we've discussed, a better strategy is to write rich, relevant content that connects with customers, solves a problem, offers insightful info, or highlights a benefit you offer that can help with a pain point.

Leave the stuffing for Thanksgiving. It has no place on your website or blog.

Keyword Hierarchy

We've touched upon keyword hierarchy a couple of times in the book. Let's recap and expand on the topic. As mentioned in Chapter 1, you don't want to have just one keyword phrase that you hammer on ad nauseam. Instead, you will want to create well-rounded list of keyword phrases for every web page and blog post. Depending on the topic and the length of the content, this list could be 3-5 keyword phrases long, or over a dozen.

No matter the length of the list, the important thing is to make sure every single phrase is relevant to the topic, service or product being "discussed" in your content. This is sometimes referred to as topic-based SEO, but I just call it good writing. For instance, if you're a pet food store that caters to dogs, well-written copy isn't just going to talk about "dog food." You're also going to talk about dog food for puppies and for older dogs. You'll want to talk about different breeds of dogs and what foods might be best for them — and don't forget dog treats! In addition, how the foods you sell relate to overall canine health and dental health are relevant, organic topics you might want to talk about. You get the idea. Well-rounded is good for the human eye — and for SEO.

Primary, Secondary & Semantic Keywords

Once you've developed your list of keywords for a particular web page of blog post, you'll need to decide which phrases are primary, secondary and semantic, respectively:

- *Primary keywords* are exactly what you'd think: They are the main keywords you'll use on a page. Sometimes you'll decide on your primary keywords in advance, and other times your organically written content will dictate them for you. Regardless, your primary keywords are the very best keywords you can find to implement into the content you're working on.

I recommend using your primary keywords approximately 8–12 times on a page of average length (500–600 words). If your content is on the shorter side, this might not be possible, and that's OK. If your content is 1,500 words long — if you're writing a "deep-dive" blog post, for example — it's perfectly natural for the primary keyword count to go up. No matter what the length of your content, make sure it reads like natural, well-written copy. Remember, we want to avoid stuffing.

- *Secondary keywords* are used less often than primary keywords and play a secondary role in optimizing the page. On average, you can expect to use a secondary keyword 3–6 times, depending on the overall length of your content. An average-length page will come closer to 3 iterations, and longer content will be closer to 6.

- *Semantic keywords* are used only 1–2 times at most, but they still play an important role in "rounding out" the relevance of the content.

Semantic and secondary keywords play a supporting role in the optimization of content. They're good to use, but they don't have the oomph that a main keyword has, typically for three reasons: 1) they have low search numbers; 2) they have high competition; 3) they're not the main topic of the page but work tangentially to support the main topic. Someone who's novice at SEO may use secondary and semantic keywords as their main keywords or may overlook them completely.

The Baseball Glove Analogy
The truth is, using semantic keywords can sometimes unite a web page in a way that Google really likes — helping improve its authority and ranking in search results. Think about it: Would you rather read an article that repeated the same keyword phrases over and over? Or would you prefer one that offered variety and nuance?

A good way to picture how this works is to compare primary, secondary and semantic keywords to a baseball glove. We've all seen a baseball glove, right?

Primary keywords are like the main parts of the glove: the pocket, the web, the fingers and thumb. Without them, you don't have a glove.

Your secondary and semantic keywords are the **stitching** that holds the glove together. Without the stitching, if you try to catch a ball, it will probably fall through the glove — *because the stitching is what brings the main parts of the glove together*, making a cohesive whole.

Ensuring every web page and blog post contains primary, secondary and semantic keywords can go a long way in helping improve your website's authority and ranking.

6. Descriptive Links
We've talked a lot about content, and technically we're not done yet because descriptive links, also referred to as text links, are part of your content.

Text links are typically links that ask visitors to take action — to learn more, schedule an appointment, make a purchase, and so on. Like the other areas we're focusing on here, this one needs to be optimized. Simply stating something like "learn more," misses an opportunity to give Google — and your reader — good, clear information.

A well-crafted text link should include at least one keyword phrase whenever possible. Once again using our fictitious Caffeinated Dentist website as an example, let's say we want to create a text link on the root-canal page to encourage visitors to schedule a consultation. Instead of simply saying, "schedule a consultation," we can add in a relevant keyword phrase (taken from our keyword report) so the text link reads, "schedule a root canal consultation." This adds SEO value to the text link, which in turn increases the page's credibility — typically referred to as authority.

A Word — or Two — About Meta Descriptions

Crafting unique meta descriptions for each of your web pages and blog posts can improve the page's clarity and user experience — as well as increase your credibility.

If you're not familiar with the term, meta descriptions are the short paragraphs Google shows as part of its search results. Like this ...

Cuppa SEO: SEO Services Madison WI | Web Design Agency | UX
https://www.cuppaseo.com/ ▾
Based in Madison, WI, Cuppa SEO offers SEO, web design & Adwords services that get you found, build trust & make it easy for visitors to become customers.

It's important to know that meta descriptions are only for the human eye; they have no SEO value. In other words, meta descriptions don't affect search engine ranking. But they're still important, because when they're well written, they can evoke a feeling of trust and peace of mind. If people are reading one of your meta descriptions, it's your first (and possibly only) chance to engage with them.

Until recently, meta descriptions could be only a maximum of 156 characters long (including spaces). If you went past that character count, you'd see an ellipsis at the end of the meta description.

Google now allows up to 300 characters (including spaces). Because I don't see consistency from Google with this yet, if you can still fit what you have to say in 156 characters or less, it might be a good idea to stick with that for now to make sure you're not getting cut short by an ellipsis.

Make sure your meta descriptions are clear, engaging — and the correct length!

THE SANDWICH ANALOGY

As you can see, there are many layers to optimizing a web page. In many ways, it's like a sandwich.

Think about it for a moment: Two pieces of bread can sustain life, right? But I don't know anybody who wants to have two pieces of bread for breakfast, lunch and dinner.

Instead, if we create a gourmet sandwich — organic turkey, lettuce, tomato, mayo or mustard, a pickle on the side — along with your favorite drink, now you've got something that's got layer-after-layer of deliciousness, making it much more palatable than two pieces of bread.

It's the same with your website. Any live site can be like two pieces of bread. It doesn't have to be optimized or have relevant content on it. As long as someone has the correct URL, they can get there. But this type of site may not be so appealing to Google or to your potential customers. Much like two pieces of bread as a meal, nobody is going to look forward to visiting your site. And Google certainly won't want to refer people to it.

But once you start adding in all of those SEO layers we spoke about, you have a sandwich that's palatable to both Google and the human eye.

Consider this: Your content is like the organic turkey. Your optimized images are like the lettuce. Your headlines are like the fresh tomato, and so on. Tell me, is your mouth watering a bit right now? If so, good! That's exactly the effect we want to have on Google — and people — with every web page and blog post we create.

One question remains: is it time for lunch, yet?

Next Steps
1. Assess your website's SEO in the six key areas we covered.
2. Review your content's richness and relevance.
3. Give it an honest grade of A through D- (nobody gets an F here).
4. Create a keyword report, or hire someone to create one for you.
5. Optimize every nook and cranny of your website and blog.

SEO BEYOND IMPLEMENTATION

Now that we've thoroughly examined the implementation process, let's address a few items that can have a positive or negative effect on your SEO efforts. To begin, let's examine your mobile website and answer the following question ...

Is Your Website Mobile Friendly?

Since April of 2015, Google has placed SEO significance on whether or not a website is mobile friendly. Over time, being mobile friendly has become more and more important, both for a website's SEO value *AND* the overall user experience visitors have on your mobile site. In the UX section of the book, we'll talk all about how to improve your mobile site's UX.

Here, we'll focus here on how the SEO value of a site is affected by whether or not it's mobile friendly.

To begin, let's assess if your website is mobile friendly:

View Your Site on a Mobile Device

How does it look? This is what I like to call the eyeball test, and it's pretty accurate. If your site isn't mobile friendly, it may look something like this:

This is a bit of an extreme example, but as of this writing, the mobile screenshot you see here is still LIVE for this company. Ewww ...

In comparison, a mobile-friendly site will look like this:

Big difference, right? And although the results are blatantly obvious without testing, I encourage you to do a mobile-friendly test anyway. It's quick, free and provided by Google.

Take the Google Mobile-friendly Test

To make sure your mobile web design is meeting Google's standards, simply take its mobile-friendly test: www.google.com/webmasters/tools/mobile-friendly/. Once there, enter your full homepage URL (web address). When you get the results, you should also test a subpage URL as well. Google will tell you if you've passed or flunked.

Holistic Side Note: Even if your site DOES pass Google's test, ask yourself if your web design offers a good user experience (UX) for your visitors, and if it has a clear call-to-action (CTA) that leads those visitors to the next step you want them to take. More on both of these points later ...

Are you Depending on Your Website for More Business?

If so, what percentage? The reason I ask is simple. If you DO depend on your website to gain business, it's imperative that you make it mobile friendly ASAP. Google is making it harder for non-mobile-friendly sites to get found. If you DON'T depend on your website for business, then it may not be as imperative to make it mobile friendly.

Talk with Your Web Designer

Ask your designer what it will take to make your site mobile friendly and what you can expect from the mobile site once it is mobile friendly with regards to aesthetic, UX and conversion. This is an important question because mobile-friendly web design is often more than simply making a site responsive (so it's adjustable to any screen size). It's also about ensuring that the hierarchy of the mobile pages makes sense for a good user experience AND conversion. This is exactly how Cuppa SEO addresses every website we work on. Make sure your web developer does the same.

Top 10 Google Panda Do's and Don'ts

Have you heard of Google Panda?

He's very smart. And although he's cute, you don't want to get on his bad side. Simply put, Google Panda is an algorithm that filters websites into two main groups — sites it likes and sites it doesn't like. The sites that Panda "likes" are upgraded in Google's search results, and the ones it doesn't like get downgraded.

Why You Should Care

If your website is breaking some of Panda's rules, your ranking could plummet, making it harder for you to connect with customers. If you adhere to Panda's rules and implement the SEO strategies outlined in this book, you'll be in much better shape.

Here's a top-ten list of Panda do's and don'ts:

DO

- Make sure you have original content on all your pages.

- On that note, keep in mind that original and *boring* won't cut it with human eyes or the eyes of Google Panda. Your content has to be engaging and interesting — offering value and relevance to the reader, which is often referred to as "rich" content. Panda hates pages that have been created for the sole purpose of increasing traffic. Instead, Panda fancies pages that are full of relevant content, written with "passion." Yes, algorithms are now smart enough to know (for the most part) if you're posting with sincerity or if you're just greedy for more traffic.

- Use keywords optimally, as we've discussed. Proper keyword selection and implementation play a significant role in where you'll rank.

- Use the SEO tool we talked about earlier (KWFinder.com), or something of similar quality to help you choose the best keywords and keyword phrases for your Keyword Report. And make sure you have a good understanding of how to use whatever tool you choose before your start to create the report.

- Learn about your customers. What are they looking for? What problems do they need solved? What solutions can you offer them through your website or blog? Relevant answers to these questions will help you write engaging content. It will also help you create your keyword report.

DON'T

- Lift content from other websites. Nicely put, this is called duplicate content — honestly put, this is plagiarism. Either way, it's a rule breaker. Instead, write your own content.

- Cut corners on keywords or quality content. A successful SEO strategy entails taking the time you need to create pages that are well-written and well-optimized.

- Be boring. If a web page is boring to you, it's probably boring to everyone else (including Google Panda).

- Create web pages with the mindset of getting more traffic. Instead, create web pages that offer value people can get excited about. You will get more traffic AND more business. Plus, Google Panda will like you.

- Use too many keywords. Stuffing is another big rule breaker.

Are Your Backlinks Google Penguin Compliant?

Now officially part of the Google Panda algorithm, Google Penguin can have a direct effect on your website authority. I often find that there's confusion — or an overall lack of knowledge — about Penguin.

You need to understand what Google Penguin is, what it has to do with backlinks (we'll define those too), and how it can affect how well — or poorly — your website ranks.

What is Google Penguin?
My wife and I absolutely love penguins. Always have. In fact, at our wedding we had life-size, wind-up penguins we released onto the dance floor. They were cute, harmless, and everybody liked them.

As far as Google Penguin is concerned, there's nothing intrinsically not to like UNLESS you're breaking the rules it's asking you to follow. Penguin doesn't care if you're breaking the rules on purpose — or by accident — so it's important to understand what it's asking of you.

As I mentioned, Penguin is part of Google's suite of ranking algorithms. In plain terms, it's part of the software that determines where your website ranks in natural search results. One of Penguin's main purposes is to identify websites that are trying to manipulate search results through the use of *sketchy backlink initiatives*.

If you're not familiar with the term, a backlink is a link from somebody else's website or blog to yours. Backlinks are important because they have the ability to raise or lower your website authority in a meaningful way, depending on the quality of the backlinks you attain. I say "depending on the quality," because not all backlinks are created equal.

Bad Types of Backlinks
- Paid links, which is a link that's actually paid for (with money, a favor, gifts, etc.).

- Link networking, which occurs when two websites trade links, or link to each other in order to boost backlink numbers.

- Links from overly spammy sites. A good way to check for site spamminess is to use an application like MOZ's Open Site Explorer (https://moz.com/researchtools/ose/). Its free to use, and it will tell you the spam score of any website for which you are considering creating a backlink. You can also check sites that have already added a backlink to your website (with or without your permission) to check their spam score. While you're there, check your site's spam score, too!

Good Types of Backlinks
- Sharing a link, or someone sharing a link to you, because it's great information that's relevant to readers

- Links that come from reputable websites — with low spam scores and high authority scores (sites that have higher authority scores than your site are preferable)

- Backlinks that require some amount of editorial control. Examples include: guest blogging, directory submissions (citations), press release distribution, blog commenting, niche forums and community sites. All of these are editorially controlled (gaited). In other words, someone has to approve or reject the submission as opposed to simply being submitted and accepted (non-gaited).

Holistic Side Note: You may be wondering what citations are, as the term has more than one meaning. In this case, we're talking about website citations, which are essentially directory listings for your website.

They're important, and luckily easy to build upon, especially if you use an application such as Bright Local (https://www.brightlocal.com). Bright Local helps you identify where you already have citations, suggests potential new citations, and SUBMITS these citations for you so you can spend your time doing something else.

My goal for this section is to raise your awareness so you'll be careful about how your backlinks are handled — and who handles them. For example, if someone offers to increase your backlinks by hundreds or thousands in a short amount of time, that person is probably practicing questionable strategies to do so. And that can mean trouble for your website.

In fact, large amounts of backlinks created in a brief amount of time can look suspicious to Google. If this happens, your efforts can actually work against your website, so build your backlinks carefully and with patience. According to Bright Local, "citation building should appear *natural* to the search engines and be built gradually over the course of a few months. A good figure to work on is around 25-50 citations per month." We're sometimes even more cautious with clients, rolling out about 10 new citations every 3–4 weeks. Why? If anything looks unnatural to Google, a penalty could ensue. And if we're building a brand-new website, nothing says "unnatural" more than 500 backlinks cropping up just days after a site goes live.

Beyond citations, there are other ways to legitimately increase your backlinks — natural editorial links and manual outreach, for example. But no matter how you slice it, it's a long-term process.

If you'd like to dive deeper into it yourself, check out these articles:

- Google's Gary Illyes on Penguin: When Is It Coming and What Will It Do?, by Mark Traphagen (http://tinyurl.com/h9s5wgs)

- An In-Depth Guide to Link Quality, Link Penalties and Bad Links, by David McSweeney (https://ahrefs.com/blog/bad-links/)

- The Noob-friendly Guide to Link Building, also by David McSweeney (https://ahrefs.com/blog/link-building/)

You may have recognized what I just did. I offered backlinks to three great pieces of content — not because there's anything in it for me, but because they contain great information I want to share. Now that's a good backlink!

Because these links are in a book, they won't hold any backlink value for Mark and David. But if they appeared in a blog post, they'd be tried-and-true backlinks, and both Mark and David would be getting a little extra authority on their sites because I shared their articles with you. = ^)

The Need for Speed: Improving Your Website's Page Load Time
Did you know that in addition to on-page SEO strategies — optimizing your title tags, headlines and images, for example — there are also off-page strategies that can improve the SEO and the user experience of your website?

The strategies we'll be discussing here all fall under the umbrella of improving your website's page load time (as you may have guessed from the title of this section). And they're important for two big reasons ...

1. When someone does a search on Google, Google wants to connect that person with results that are highly relevant AND that provide a good user experience. In this case, the user experience we're referring to is *speed* ...

2. When someone arrives on your website, their expectation is not to wait around for 5 or more seconds while your 5mb images load.

They have the need for speed (like Lightning McQueen), and rightly so. A web page that loads quickly is simply a better experience, right?

So to satisfy Google (and get a bump in website authority), and to satisfy visitors (and get a bump in UX), the first thing you need to do is perform a Google Speed Test on your website.

This is actually super easy. Just cut and paste your URL into the field on Google's Page Speed Test (https://developers.google.com/speed/pagespeed/insights/). Typically, you'll get an almost instant answer as to how well the page you entered is optimized.

Once you get your score (which can vary slightly each time you do the test), all you need to do to make improvements is follow Google's PageSpeed Insights Rules, which are ...

- Avoid landing page redirects
- Enable compression
- Improve server response time
- Leverage browser caching
- Minify resources
- Optimize images
- Optimize CSS Delivery
- Prioritize visible content
- Remove render-blocking JavaScript

At first glance, this is probably externally overwhelming (unless you're a web developer). But these are all very manageable steps for a competent web developer to implement.

The result? Higher optimization scores from Google, and faster load time for visitors. We did this on the Cuppa SEO website a while back and were able to attain some very high optimization numbers: 93% on mobile devices, and 94% on desktop.

If you're interested in learning more on how to improve your site's page load time, visit Google's PageSpeed Insights Rules page — https://developers.google.com/speed/docs/insights/rules.

Are Your Images as Big As Godzilla?

I know, the first thing you thought about when you woke up today was the size of the images on your website, right? Or maybe that was just me ...

Regardless of how off-the-radar this topic may be for you, it's an important one because image file size (KB, MB, GB) can affect site speed, which in turn has a direct impact on your SEO. The good news is that if you have a WordPress site, there are plugins that can help you optimize image file size automatically.

How Image File Size Works

Every time you load an image to your website, it has a certain file size (which is different from how big your image renders on you site). The bigger the file size (typically in KB or MB), the longer the image takes to load on your site.

For instance, if you've had professional team member photos taken, and the actual file size of each image is about 5MB, that's fine if you're going to print the photos, but it's bad news if you place photos of that size on your website.

Image Optimization Software

Enter the image optimizer, which can automatically lower the overall footprint of each image's file size. We typically use an image optimizer called Short Pixel, but there are others out there.

What's nice about Short Pixel is the cost is low, and it works in the background so you don't have to worry about it.

Here's an Example of How it Works

The file size of an image for one of my blog posts (before I ran it through Short Pixel) was 184 KB ...

> File name: **SEO-Tips-Optimize-Image-File-Size.jpg**
>
> File type: **JPG**
>
> File size: **184 KB**
>
> Dimensions: **800 × 457**

The file size was reduced 34.81% once it was processed ...

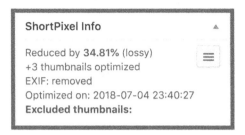

Nice!

This results in faster load time, which provides a better user experience for your visitors. Google also likes fast load time and will give you an SEO bump when it sees that your site is fast (as we learned a little earlier).

Lossy vs. Lossless
There are two major options when setting up your image optimization software:

1. *Lossy compression*: This provides the highest compression rate, which means it makes your image file size as small as possible while still looking good (for the most part). According to applications like Short Pixel, "this is the recommended option for most users, producing results that look the same as the original to the human eye." This is what we typically use to reduce image file size.

2. *Lossless compression*: this provides a compressed image that is "pixel-identical" with the original image — so no image quality is lost. As you can imagine, this option does not minimize the footprint of your image as much as lossy, which means load time could be higher with lossless.

Holistic Side Note: I mentioned "for the most part" in option #1, because we've found that if there is text in your imagery (as with a screenshot of a web page), lossy compression can make the image look blurred and pixelated. Definitely review your images once you've processed them to make sure they look good on a high-resolution display — a MacBook Pro retina display or an iPad, for example. And if your image is text heavy (like the screenshots on Cuppa SEO's Web Design Gallery page), it might be better to set your compression to lossless before uploading.

Optimized file image size is an all-around win for your website, bringing a better user experience to visitors and making Google happy, too!

The Rise of HTTPS
Back in November of 2017 Google rolled out some changes regarding HTTP and HTTPS on their Chrome web browser.

This change made it important for every business to seriously consider switching their site over to HTTPS — because Google has informed us that HTTPS is now a ranking signal (still considered a small one as of 2017, among dozens of others).

In case you're not familiar with the acronyms:

- HTTP = Hypertext Transfer Protocol
- HTTPS = Secure Hypertext Transfer Protocol

You've probably seen both of these in front of countless URLs (although sometimes they're hidden depending on your web browser).

HTTPS has been a must for any site that's conducting financial transactions or handling sensitive information of any kind. Until recently, sites that didn't fit these categories were OK with being HTTP.

Here at Cuppa SEO, we've been building sites with HTTPS for years, simply because it makes sense to have an added level of security in place.

It now has become more mandatory.

As of October 2017, if you didn't comply, you'd see a little **"i"** in a circle to the left of your URL:

This is obviously Levi's U.S. website. The little **"i"** in the circle is the place where Google informs the viewer that the site (or at least this page), is not "secure." In other words, some of Levis' non-transactional pages are now being flagged as unsecure by Google Chrome ...

Up until July 2018, the info you see in the pop-up box above showed only when you clicked on the little **"i,"** which means most of the general public probably won't take much notice.

That said, as soon as you go to make a purchase, it's completely secure, so it's not like Levi's is putting a customer's credit card and personal info in jeopardy. But Google is looking to protect additional information — the info you enter into a contact form or to sign up for a newsletter, for example.

(Note: As of July 2018, Levi's site appears to be completely HTTPS.)

But wait, there's more (thanks Google). As of July 2018, that harmless **"i"** has some company ...

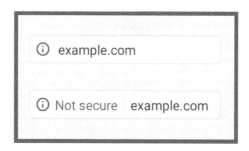

Now it's blatantly obvious when a site is not HTTPS, and the statement "not secure" can easily undermine a visitor's confidence in your website and your brand.

SEO and Website Authority

Chrome is NOT the only web browser that applies this type of aesthetic change ("secure" versus "unsecure") on every website URL. In Safari, you'll see a little lock next to the URL when it's secure. Same with Firefox.

Because I'm on a Mac, I can't see what Internet Explorer displays, but I'm betting it's something similar. How the July 2018 "not secure" change will play out on non-Chrome browsers remains to be seen, but you don't have to worry about it if your site is HTTPS. You have other questions to consider: What's happening in the Google algorithm? What website authority implications does this have for HTTP and HTTPS sites? In less than a year, Google has tightened the screws on security in a big way, which leads me to believe it will only tighten them further with penalties if you're not HTTPS compliant.

As mentioned earlier, this was considered a "small ranking signal" in 2017. Back then, I realized this mirrored the mobile-friendly trend that Google implemented a few years back (remember mobilegeddon?). In less than a year, HTTPS has become more than a small ranking signal, and I believe this trend will only continue.

Bottom line: If you don't already have a true HTTPS website, talk with your web developer about making it one. In many cases, it doesn't take long to implement, and it's better to be on the safe side so you don't receive penalties from Google or lose credibility with visitors. And because HTTPS will give you an SEO bump (which may or may not be noticeable), it could have ranking benefits that might bear more fruit in the future.

6. User Experience (UX)

In Part 1 of the book, we defined user experience. Now it's time to apply those learnings right into your website.

As mentioned earlier, we'll be taking a heuristic approach to analyzing and optimizing the user experience on sample websites, offering you hands-on, in-the moment learning on how to apply a great UX to your own site. Specifically, you'll learn how to assess the user experience of every page of your site for desktop and obile, respectively, including reviewing the hierarchy of each page for:

- UX and website navigation (architecture)
- Homepage and subpage layout (aesthetic)
- Optimal placement of elements such as images, copy, and calls-to-action (CTAs)

UX AND WEBSITE NAVIGATION: DESKTOP
When it comes to site navigation (nav), it's always a good idea to be as clear as possible. Like the Dollar Shave Club homepage example at right, you need to ensure that your navigation makes sense and involves zero guesswork. In other words, this is not the place to be cute or metaphorical.

As you can see, Dollar Shave Club ensures that everything is clear in its main navigation. "Our Blades," "Our Products," and "Gift," all tell you exactly where you'll land when you click on them. "How it Works," "Reviews" and "Account" do the same. Crystal clear, right?

The only not-so-clear component of the Dollar Share Club navigation is "Box." This is actually what's going to be contained in your next shipment, or box, but it's not necessarily clear what this is until you've become a customer.

But wait, there's more (unfortunately). Dollar Shave Club also has a secondary "sandwich" navigation. You can see it just to the left of where it says "Menu."

When you click on "Menu," the secondary navigation opens up ...

As you can see, the hierarchy of the secondary navigation is identical to the primary navigation, which is good.

But here's the question: Why is this secondary navigation here at all? What is its purpose? In terms of UX, it adds another element to the page. And from what we've learned, the more elements a page has, the more site visitors have to think. The more visitors have to think, the better the chance they'll get distracted from what you want them to do.

On one hand, when the secondary navigation is collapsed, it's non-obtrusive. But, again, **why is it there?**

There are only two differences between the secondary navigation and the primary navigation:

1. The products are all laid out nice and neat in the secondary navigation. But ... this could also be accomplished by creating a dropdown menu in the primary navigation under the "Products" tab.

2. There is a solitary item in the secondary navigation that doesn't appear in the primary navigation: "Original Content." This is the Dollar Shave Club blog, which could easily be added to the primary

navigation as "Blog," rendering the secondary navigation useless in the process — which would make site visitors' user experiences even better.

Regarding point #2, Dollar Shave Club forgot the "be crystal clear" rule when it got a little cute/metaphorical with the name of the blog, "Original Content." Because you're on a shaving site, you should be able to pretty much assume that the content is going to be about shaving and male-related topics. But *original content* could be a lot of things — like a book or the latest HULU original TV show — so why not just call it what it is, a blog?

These may seem like small points. But how many ambiguous things does it take to make your visitor confused? Anything that is even remotely confusing needs to be made clear or removed.

When it comes to the user experience, if there's a simpler way, then do it. In this case, the simpler way is painfully simple, *AND OBVIOUS*.

One Navigation
As you can see, whenever possible it's always best to have ONE site navigation. For a large portion of websites, a single navigation with a drop-down menu will suffice nicely.

If you have a more-complex page hierarchy on your website, it may be necessary to:

- Have a primary navigation with a drop-down menu
- Have a secondary navigation for your subpages (see J. Crew example below)

Drop-down Menu Example
Cuppa SEO has a single navigation with a drop-down menu that looks like this:

A cascading menu appears when you hover over one of the primary drop-down choices. In this case, my cursor was hovering over "Web Design":

In the following example, my cursor was hovering over "Search Engine Optimization (SEO)":

To keep the UX clean and easy for the user to digest, the cascading menu should be in alignment with whatever service or product it's expanding upon.

To further clarify what the secondary drop-down is associated with, it's helpful to have the primary dropdown that's being hovered over change color. On the Cuppa SEO site, this color change is subtle and does not translate well to print. I've enhanced it here so you can see what I mean:

Holistic Side Note: Cascading menus aren't always the first choice when it comes to navigation solutions. What I've found is, like everything else, the decision for best type of navigation needs to be decided in context. Yes, the cascading menu needs to be developed in a way that is easy to use (glitchy menus of ANY kind can be very frustrating), but I've found it to sometimes be a better solution than implementing a left-side navigation or a mega menu.

In the Case of Cuppa SEO's website, the latter two options would be overkill, which is why we went with the cascading menu. In other cases, like the ones we're about to examine, a mega menu and/or left-side navigation are the superior choice.

Other Types of Navigation
If you're housing dozens — or even hundreds — of product pages, a mega menu can help provide a solid UX. Let's take a look at Williams-Sonoma's website as an example ...

Or if you simply *must* have a secondary navigation, make sure it's consistent on every page of your site as is J. Crew's in this side-navigation example:

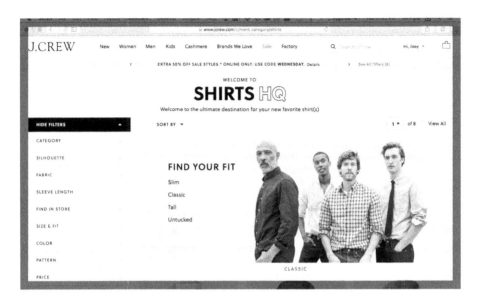

Some sites are selective about when the secondary navigation appears or is removed from a page, which can cause confusion and leave the visitor feeling stranded or lost (bad UX).

With Dollar Shave Club, there wasn't an obvious reason for the secondary navigation's existence. But in the case of J. Crew, the secondary navigation is used wisely. It's on EVERY landing page for every product category (Men, Women, Kids, etc.) for a specific reason: to help clarify what the buyer's options are WITHIN that particular product category without having to use the primary navigation.

And with J. Crew, there are so many product pages that when site visitors drill down to the section they want to be in, having the secondary navigation available on the left side of the page actually improves the user experience. The secondary navigation acts as an at-a-glance guide for options that exist *within that product category*. In other words, it's clarifying the situation and placing the visitor on solid ground.

As you can see, the secondary navigation is NOT present on the homepage …

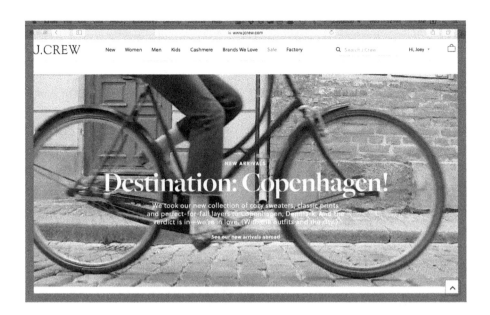

This is not an oversight. The secondary navigation has been removed with good reason: The visitor has not yet provided information about the product category in which he or she might have interest. And since the secondary navigation is meant to provide easy clarification about where you might want to go next *within a specific product category*, there's no use for it on the homepage.

DESKTOP NAVIGATION GONE WRONG
Multiple navigations or primary and secondary navigations can be tricky and difficult for a user to navigate, resulting in a bad user experience.

Let's take a look at a site with a multi-navigation hierarchy so you can see what I mean ...

As you can see, there are at least FIVE different navigations in this homepage example. Let's examine each.

Navigation #1 & #2
In the above example, #1 is the primary navigation. Then you've got #2, a secondary navigation above it.

Already, the user's focus is split — at least for a few seconds, which can be enough to confuse or distract someone. These choices do not achieve the desired effect.

Navigation #3
But this website isn't done yet. The third navigation (#3) sits above the secondary navigation: the search box and social buttons. It's typically a bad idea to place social buttons at the top of a web page like this for two reasons:

- Social buttons add another layer of navigation to the site. Now the user's focus is split into three.

- What is the purpose of those social buttons? To take someone to one of your social media platforms, right? As we'll see in Part 4 of this book, social media more often is a tool that helps drive people TO YOUR WEBSITE.

When you place your social buttons at the top of your page, your risk competing with your primary navigation — and directing someone AWAY from your website.

When we have drawn someone on our website, the last thing we want to do is have them leave! We'll revisit this in Part 4, but I wanted to touch on it briefly here.

Navigation #4
Navigation #4 is an advertisement for Advil. And although it's not technically part of the navigation (it's a call-to-action), I'm counting it here because it is taking up prime real estate where your primary navigation should be!

Navigation #5
This navigation sits mid-page, disjointed from the primary navigation. Navigation #5 contains news-centric information, something that could easily be communicated through adding "News" to the primary navigation, along with a drop down menu to accommodate each tab.

At this point, the visitor's focus has potentially been split five times — and that's not even counting the slider they use for multiple hero images (bad for UX) and the other links and calls-to-action on the page.

Holistic Side Note: Although it's obvious that too many navigation menus are a poor UX, I don't want to lose sight of the fact that it IS a UX best practice to provide more than one path to the most important information on a website. This can be done in a variety of ways, and needs to be examined case-by-case for the best solution. Because of this, we won't dive into it here, but it's a concept worth keeping in mind.

UX & WEBSITE NAVIGATION: MOBILE
Just when you thought we were probably done talking about navigation, I spring mobile nav on you. Mobile navigation needs just as much attention as desktop navigation. Luckily, the same principles apply, but they look different because we're on a different platform.

Here are a handful of examples of mobile navigation with an excellent UX.

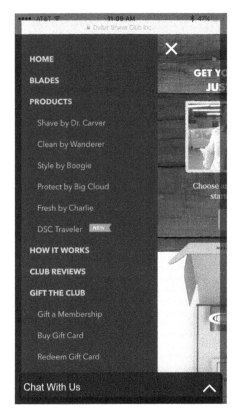 

The example on the left is from the Dollar Shave Club mobile site. The example on the right is from the Lighthouse Healing Massage therapy site (built by Cuppa SEO).

In both cases, the navigation follows a clear, easy-to-digest hierarchy.

If you have multiple services or products, you can implement an accordion-style mobile navigation — a nice touch that expands and contracts when there's a dropdown menu. Here's what this looks like on the Cuppa SEO site.

On the left is an example of the collapsed navigation. On the right is an example of the expanded navigation, which is triggered when you click "Services."

Mega Menus and Left-side Navigation on Mobile

As we saw with J. Crew's desktop site, mega menus and/or side-navigations can provide an excellent solution for creating a clear navigational hierarchy on a complex site. But, because of smaller screen size, these solutions don't work on mobile devices like smartphones.

Let's take a look at Banana Republic's mobile site to see how they deal with a smaller screen size that doesn't allow for a mega menu or left-side navigation — while still maintaining a clear navigational hierarchy.

When you tap the sandwich nav on Banana Republic's mobile homepage, a menu appears offering top-level options like "Men," "Women," etc. ...

Choosing "Men" drills down to more specific options that all live under the men's category ...

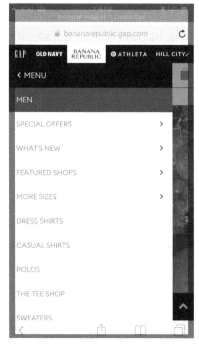

Did you notice what happened to the menu after "Men" was chosen?
- A new choice, "Menu" appears at the top of the navigation with a black background.
- "Men" now has a dark grey background color.
- Right away, Banana Republic is setting us up for success with color coding that is actually a form of a "breadcrumb trail," so we always know where we're at in the nav.

Choosing "Special Offers" drills down to reveal more options, as well as another level of color coding ...

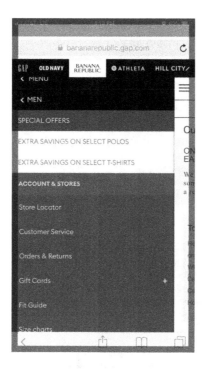

As we drill deeper into the men's section, and are provided with more specific choices, our progression remains clear because of the color coding ...
- In the screenshot above, "Men" and "Menu" are both black, and include an arrow pointing to the left. These visual cues convey that anything black is a back button that will bring you to exactly where you expect to go (in this case, the main menu or the main men's section).
- "Special Offers" turns dark grey showing you exactly where you currently are.

- "Extra Savings on Select Polos," and "Extra Savings on Select T-Shirts," have a white background — drawing the eye to them, and making it obvious that these are the available next choices for Special Offers (from the very beginning, anything white has been a clickable option).
- This simple, yet well thought out color-coding system helps visitors understand exactly where they are in the navigation hierarchy — which is good UX because it helps us keep our bearings at all times.

Holistic Side Note: The color coding can't take all the credit for the clarity of this mobile navigation. The straightforward wording used in each navigation tab plays a large role, too.

When we choose "Extra Savings on Select Polos," we're taken to a subpage that contains actual product.

This page contains a real UX win because it allows users to navigate in two ways:

1. Tapping on the sandwich nav in the upper left-hand corner. This is like a hard reset, though, bringing us back to the beginning of the navigation journey.
2. Tapping the on-page "Filter" button that allows us to refine the options for the section we're currently in ...

Here, we can really get specific about what we're looking for. The "Category" filter is worth a closer look.

If we pick "Category," we're able to choose one or more filters to make our search results even more specific. Note how all options are polo-centric. Why? Because Banana Republic is keeping the focus on what you told them you were interested in, as opposed to opening the category choices up to a wider variety of options. This is a way to make website visitors feel grounded and comfortable about where they are — for a solid UX every step of the way.

NAVIGATION HIERARCHY
The final point I'd like to cover regarding navigation is the order in which your tabs should appear.

It can be tempting to lead with your About section, just after your Home tab, but it's not the optimal place for it. Businesses often feel it's important that potential customers know their history and what they're about. But if you remember when we talked about content in Part 1 of the book, this information is often less important to the customer. What they care about is their pain points being addressed.

Keith Gilmore, a conversion expert, once told me a story about a man who broke his arm and was rushed to the hospital. When he got to the emergency room, the doctor began telling him about her credentials — where she went to school, when she graduated, the different hospitals and private practice's she's worked at over the years, and how many broken bones she's set back into place.

Now, do you think for one second that the patient cared about any of this? That patient is sitting there IN PAIN, and he wants the doctor to fix his pain.

Just as you need to keep your content customer-centric, the same holds true for your navigation.

Instead of a navigation that's ordered like this ...

Make your nav look like this ...

In the first example, you're offered to check out "About," "Why Artisan," *and a "Tour,"* before you get to the services they provide. Yes, it only takes a few seconds to find the "Services" tab, but why unnecessarily diminish the UX in your navigation? Remember, most people look for services or products when they're in some kind of pain. Address their pain!

> **Social Side Note:** *Notice that the former navigation example also includes social buttons right in the navigation. Would you want to check out a dentist's Facebook page if you needed a root canal? Although there are some cases where use of social buttons can actually be helpful (as we'll see shortly), in most cases, they won't prove helpful as part of your navigation — or your conversion strategy for that matter.*

The second example is from one of our client's websites, Roger Wolkoff, and of course it provides the "Programs" and "Event Planners" tabs right up at the front of the navigation — making it all about potential customers/ clients and why they're visiting the site in the first place.

For most websites, the following navigation hierarchy will help provide a solid UX.

If you're a products-based company, just place Products where you currently see Services listed. If you have both products and services, decide which is more important and lead with that.

If you believe your navigation needs to be different, identify WHY it needs to be different. For example, if you're a professional speaker, your Video page might trump everything else, because the first thing a potential client wants to see is you presenting! If that's the case, move it to the beginning of the left side.

There's No Place Like Home
You may notice that the Cuppa SEO website navigation does not have a Home tab. Of course, this is intentional — and quite common. Typically, visitors know that if they click on your logo or company name (which is traditionally in the upper left-hand corner of a web page), they'll be taken back to the home page. Removing the Home tab makes your navigation a little shorter and a little easier to digest — both of which are good for UX.

UX AND YOUR HOMEPAGE: DESKTOP
In addition to a successful primary navigation, the Dollar Shave Club homepage also provides a solid overall user experience. The website is clean, clear and well designed, with just a couple of calls-to-action to choose from: 1) Watch the video and 2) "Do It":

The sparse copy above the CTA is clear, compelling — and expresses five great value propositions (benefits) in just 15 words:

1. A great shave
2. For a few bucks a month
3. No commitment
4. No fees
5. No BS

This is UX at its finest.

There's no need to think about it; I know exactly what the benefits are.

Sure, there are more details and choices, but this is not the place for them — and Dollar Shave Club understands that. I'm either satisfied with my current shaving solution or I'm not. And even if I am, maybe I don't like paying twenty bucks for blades every few weeks.

If some or most of these benefits sound good to me (in my case, they all did), I don't need to think — I just need to click on the "DO IT" button. Easy, pleasant and pain-free! Might their razors deliver the same value?

And if I'm not yet ready to buy? Dollar Shave Club gives me an opportunity to get to know the company and product better with a short video, no strings attached.

Holistic Side Note: In case you're wondering why we're discussing conversion in the UX section, the answer is simple. UX and conversion are enmeshed in a significant way. Any time you have a call-to-action (CTA), it's either enhancing or deterring your user experience. And just as your CTAs affect the success of your UX, your UX affects the success of your CTAs.

But enough about calls-to-action and conversion, at least for now. We'll be diving deeper into them in the next part of the book.

Social Side Note: Below the video on the homepage, Dollar Shave Club incorporates social media buttons. This is typically a no-no because we don't want to drive someone from our website to social media. Instead, we want to drive people from social media to our website! In this case, though, it actually makes a lot of sense for Dollar Shave Club to have social buttons on this page. Why? It's all about how they have the buttons set up ...

Here, Dollar Shave Club is providing what's called "social proof." On the first line, I can see that at least two of my friends have liked this brand on Facebook (along with over two million other people). That's impressive — and personalized.

The second line does the same (although it has recently been removed from the live site). It provides social proof — very strong brand validation — for Dollar Shave Club.

Dollar Shave Club also uses social media as free advertising, with social proof built right in. When I click on one of these buttons (Share, Tweet, etc.), a pop-up window appears that allows me to take the desired social action WITHOUT leaving the site. In other words, if I share Dollar Shave Club on my Facebook page, all my friends and family see it. And because they see it on MY page (hopefully a trusted person in their lives), it gains credibility.

Homepage "Hero Image" Examples

Every website we've looked at so far has some form of a "homepage hero" image. What's a "homepage hero?" It's exactly what it sounds like: the main image that typically sits close to the top of the page. Depending on your brand and your organization's goals, your hero image might take up some or all of the real estate on your homepage.

For example, on CuppaSEO.com, the hero image (also referred to as the hero shot) fills the entire screen on my 13" MacBook Pro.

There are very specific reasons why my homepage looks like this.

The biggest reason: When someone arrives at my site, I want them to feel as if they're sitting down with an longtime friend or family member — someone they can *trust* — over a cup of coffee. This is especially important in my line of work, because a lot of customers come to us after having had a bad experience elsewhere — often having spent thousands of dollars with no tangible results. Knowing a potential customer can trust us is critical, and I want to get started developing that trust immediately — as soon as they arrive at my website. Warm tones, natural wood — and a delicious cup of coffee — help accomplish this.

Another goal is to make my site as human as possible. Sure, there's plenty of tech-speak on the site, but at the end of the day, the website is simply a medium of communication between human beings. In other words, it's all about developing relationships. Just because we're doing technical, geeky work doesn't mean we forgo the relationship — especially because *the purpose of our work is to help our clients get found, connect with, and develop relationships with their clients!*

Here's another example of a homepage hero image. We created this site for our client, iMerge, with a smaller homepage hero image ...

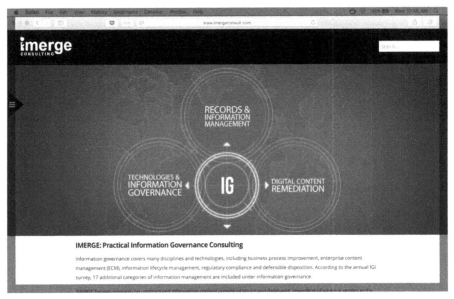

In this case, our client wanted his three calls-to-action to be built right into the image. So we created an original piece of art and overlaid interactive CTAs into the imagery.

We also wanted the headline and at least the first few lines of copy to be visible without scrolling, which is why we chose a more cinematic aesthetic for the hero image.

Finally, the client also needed the art to have an international feel (hence the map) as well as a tech vibe — which is in line with the organization. We accomplished this by how the CTAs were designed and how they glow when hovered over.

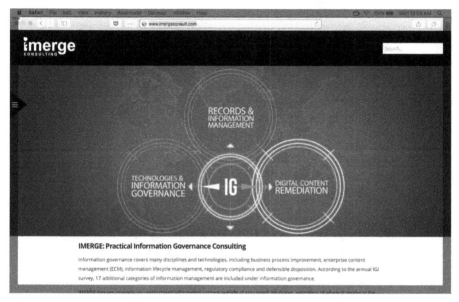

These are only two of MANY variants you could choose for your homepage hero image.

Avoid Carousels

Carousels, also referred to as slideshows or rotating offers, are something we find on a lot of websites. Caution: They're a bad user experience and they're bad for conversion.

As an organization, it's always tempting to give MORE information on one's website. But we've already discussed that more information can often have the opposite effect of what was intended.

Carousels make your visitor think harder. Every new rotating banner is new information that makes the viewer have to think, and even if it's for only a few seconds, that's a few seconds too many.

Yes, you should assume your customers are intelligent. And yes, you should also acknowledge that they're overwhelmed and super busy. As each new image or offer slides into view, you're giving them more work to do. They've got to digest it, then decide if it's more important to them than the previous image or offer(s). And then, after four slides, they're asking, "What was the first one again?" and possibly wondering how they get back to a previous offer.

Your homepage hero image, your accompanying content and your CTA should clearly address:

1. "You are here"
2. "Here's how we can help"
3. "Do this next if you want to talk"

Instead of carousels, use a single image for better UX. Then figure out the top one, two or three (maximum) things your visitors need (address those pain points), and make them easy to find calls-to-action.

Consider the iMerge CTAs we just talked about. It provides the right offers (client pain points that become your points of conversion) that are easy to find (which equals a good user experience), resulting in a more successful website. This "formula" often leads to an increase in qualified leads and a decrease in unqualified leads (more on CTAs in our next section on conversion).

The Pitfalls of Parallax Web Design

Another somewhat popular web design format is known as parallax design. Although the name might not be familiar to you, I'll bet you've experienced this type of site at least a few times.

A parallax website is often referred to as a "scrolling website." It typically comprises a single page, or just a handful of pages, with the homepage containing a TON of information.

On these scrolling websites, you start scrolling down for more info ... and down, and down, and down through what appears to be a never-ending scroll. And as you scroll, there are layers of imagery and text on the page moving at different "speeds" to create visual interest, tell a story, create the effect of depth, etc.

This type of site can be lot of fun for a designer to build, as it provides opportunities to be really creative. But it's bad for UX because it's so hard for visitors to easily locate the exact information they need. In addition, parallax sites make it hard to know which end is up. In fact, all of those moving parts may cause you to feel nauseous (I'm not kidding!).

It's almost like parachuting out of an airplane, but you've got to keep your eyes closed the whole time, so you never know where the ground is.

This can be very unsettling for viewers who are looking for "solid footing" as soon as they arrive on your site. What I mean by this is that website visitors — most of them, unconsciously — have a need to understand the lay of the land when they arrive on a website. They want to feel grounded, to be able to quickly understand where they are without having to think about it.

Because we use the Internet every day, it's easy to forget that it's a virtual platform made up of pixels that we view. To assure a good UX, we've got to provide visitors with this sense of solid footing by implementing all of the user experience strategies we've talked about thus far. They need to know "this end is up, and this end is down": solid footing on solid virtual ground. We don't want them feeling as though they're freefalling or off balance, which is exactly what often happens with parallax sites.

What follows is an example of a parallax site; it goes on and on for *nine* whopping on-screen "pages" (on a 13" Mac). Note: Horizontal lines represent scroll points, meaning you wouldn't be able to see what's below the line without scrolling ...

A Digital Agency Focused
On Growing Brands Online

We Serve All Industries

Clicking the button reveals the next "page."

After having to scroll, clicking the button reveals the next "page."

One final note about Parallax: Like anything else, there's no hard, fast "best practice" for every circumstance. I've seen some parallax sites for artists (showing one piece of art per "page"), and musicians (showing one album and/or music video per "page") that work really well. But for most businesses and organizations, there are far better choices that provide a remarkably better user experience.

The Perils of Pop-ups on Your Website

I don't know about you, but I've never known anyone who claimed to like pop-ups. Not one.

This comes as no surprise, as pop-ups on a website are a poor user experience, and they can also diminish conversion rates for the things that really matter (selling products and services).

According to my son, Joss, "Pop-ups are like whack-a-moles; you just want to smash them." I couldn't agree more. (I think we've got a UX expert in the making here!)

Pop-ups are poor for UX because they're an interruption from what people came to your site for. Plus they make a visitor have to stop to think about what the pop-up says and determine if it's relevant to them. In other words, it adds another layer of thinking and decision-making to the process — breaking the golden UX rule, "don't make me think," which was popularized by UX expert and author, Steve Krug.

And they're annoying.

Yes, pop-ups annoy visitors. Why would you want to intentionally annoy visitors when you're trying to convert them to customers? There are better ways to engage.

For instance, if the offer in your pop-up is so important, why isn't it one of your calls-to-action on your homepage? If it needs to be present beyond the homepage, consider more UX-friendly ways to integrate it into the page hierarchy. In other words, build it into an organic place where people can find it easily without having it thrown in their face.

Here's a perfect example. I was recently buying a gift for my wife's birthday. She's a yoga enthusiast, so I decided to get her some new yoga pants and tops. Every site I went to — and I do mean every site — had a pop-up with the same message: "Save 10% by signing up for our email list."

What's more important, building the email list or making a sale? If offering a discount is important to keep you competitive in the marketplace, then just provide it *without* asking me for anything in return.

Then, once I make a purchase, you could ask me if I'd like to sign up for special offers, news and discounts — after I've checked out and become a paying customer. Why do you have to ask me within the first three seconds I show up on your site — especially when your #1 conversion goal is to make a sale?

At the end of the day, a pop-up is like any other strategy on your website … it needs to be thought through carefully to ensure that it has the potential to accomplish your major goals: make a sale, schedule a consultation, etc. If it's not in direct alignment with your major goals, then either get rid of it, or figure out a way to include it as a secondary goal that's a good UX (as we suggest above, add the email sign up to the *end* of the experience).

Even if it aligns with your major goals, the questions remains: "Is this pop-up the best way to communicate with my visitor?" If it is (it's probably not), when exactly is the best time to present it so it's a good UX and not an obstacle to building a relationship?

When Chris Goward, a leading expert on conversion optimization, talks about pop-ups, he agrees that they can interrupt the visitor's experience: "Any distraction can reduce sales — especially something totally unrelated to the goal of the visit."

UX AND YOUR HOMEPAGE: MOBILE

The buzz about mobile web design, and being mobile friendly, has increased dramatically since Google started grading sites based on their "mobile-friendly factor." If you don't meet their mobile-friendly contingencies, you might get pinged, and your website authority (and ranking) could suffer.

But mobile-friendly web design has been an important UX consideration since the very first iPhone allowed people to search the Internet in the palm of their hand.

In fact, this is WHY Google rolled out its mobile-friendly initiative in the first place. The goal: Help people have the best, most relevant user experience when searching on the web. Here at Cuppa SEO, we couldn't agree more, which is why every website we build is mobile friendly, and this was the case even BEFORE Google said it had to be.

Google has reported that on a global level — on average — over 50% of search queries are performed on a mobile device. According to Hitwise, an organization that measures human behavior across mobile and desktop devices, mobile search in the United States is at approximately 58%.

Depending on country, region and industry, this percentage will vary. But overall, it's obvious that the mobile user experience you present to your viewer is important. And by the way, laptops, although highly portable, are not considered a mobile device.

So when a user searches on a mobile device for what you offer, would you prefer your site to look like this? ...

Or like this? ...

Every facet of your website should be taken into account when "going mobile" to ensure the best user experience possible — including your navigation, homepage, subpages, online store, shopping cart, etc. — which often means your mobile site has a different hierarchy than your desktop site.

Going Beyond Responsive Design
There's more to creating a truly mobile-friendly site than simply making

it responsive, which essentially means your website pages are coded to automatically resize themselves based on the screen size of the device a visitor is using. Images aren't too big or too small, and copy is always readable. In most cases, a website that includes responsive design will pass the Google mobile-friendly test.

But that doesn't mean it's providing an optimal user experience. For that, we need to go beyond responsive design and *intentionally* design the site for mobile, dictating what goes where on a page, what it looks like, what gets left out (if anything) and so on.

To clarify this point, I'd like to walk you through the aesthetic of a well-designed mobile homepage. Then we'll compare a few desktop homepages with their mobile counterparts so you can see how they differ.

Here is the Cuppa SEO mobile homepage. It contains five main strategies for a better user experience, strategies that also make your site extremely mobile friendly!

1. **Sandwich Navigation**

   Those three bars you see in the upper right-hand corner are typically referred to as sandwich navigation. They're your entire navigation collapsed into three little "bite-sized" lines, typically the optimal way to present your mobile navigation. Once the sandwich is tapped, the navigation expands and allows the viewer to choose from the full menu. Sandwich navigation typically sits above or below the hero shot (top image) on a mobile page.

2. **The Hero Shot**

   This is the main image on your mobile page. It needs to be clean, clear and clutter-free, because it has to be interpreted on a much smaller screen. For this reason, any calls-to-action you have on your desktop hero shot need to be removed for mobile. As you'll soon see, they go elsewhere.

3. **Headline**

   The main headline on any web page is called your "H1." It's the largest headline on the page, and it should live toward the top. Whenever possible, limit your headline to 2 lines of copy on mobile. It is easy to digest (good for UX), and it gives you more room for #4 and #5 on our list.

4. **Introductory Copy**

   The first couple of sentences of copy need to live here. You DON'T need to provide every little detail … at least not yet. Intro copy is meant to be just that: a brief overview of where viewers have landed so they feel they're on solid footing. This copy — and all copy on your mobile site — needs to be a large enough font for those with older eyes (or transition lenses) to easily read.

   Writers, don't dismay! The remainder of your homepage (or subpage) copy is included for mobile websites. It will just live below your …

5. **Call-to-Action (CTA)**

   In Cuppa SEO's case, we have two CTAs we want to share with visitors on our homepage: "Web Design Services," and "SEO Services." In many cases, your business may need only one call-to-action. In all cases, your CTA should drive visitors to what you want them to do next (so choose wisely). As you can see, both of my CTAs live ABOVE the scroll line, which means the viewer does not have to scroll down to see them.

All of this adds up to a user experience that viewers enjoy — and that Google defines as extremely mobile friendly.

Next Steps
If you have a website, I encourage you to view it on your smartphone to see if it's following the strategies laid out above. If not, make the necessary changes.

DESKTOP VS. MOBILE WEB DESIGN
Here are a handful of comparisons between desktop and mobile homepages. Notice how both iterations differ, yet each provides a solid UX on its respective platform.

Dollar Shave Club desktop homepage:

Dollar Shave Club mobile homepage:

Roger Wolkoff desktop homepage:

Roger Wolkoff mobile homepage:

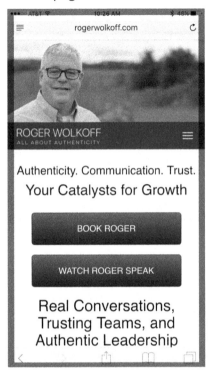

Rosy Cheeks desktop homepage:

Rosy Cheeks mobile homepage:

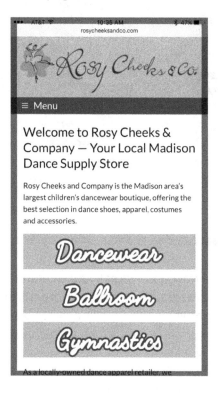

CREATING A SPECTACULAR SUBPAGE UX
Just like your homepage, subpages need to be clear and uncluttered.

Let's take a look at a handful of examples of what a great UX looks like on both desktop and mobile.

Desktop Subpage Example #1
Once again, Dollar Shave Club provides an excellent UX. On the Blades subpage, you know exactly where you are and what your options are — *without having to think about it.* Three very clear calls-to-action (my suggested maximum for any web page) make it easy to choose the blade that's right for your beard, and then to move on. The fact that the page looks clean and appealing is also important.

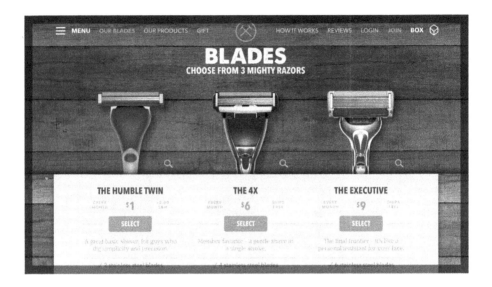

If you're a man, you know there's really no thinking involved in deciding between these three razors. Depending on the thickness of your beard, the choice is clear between the first and second option. And if you're looking for a little luxury in your life? Go with choice three.

Sure, there are lots of details below each choice, which is great for customers who want to know more. But this is OPTIONAL. I don't have to read it to make a decision. Once again, I can save my brain power for other things such as marketing my business, optimizing websites — and writing this book!

The website's user experience remains just as pleasant throughout the entire product selection and checkout process. And once you're a customer, the great UX continues.

Mobile Subpage Example #1

As you might have guessed, Dollar Shave Club's subpages provide an excellent UX. On their blades page, all three options are easily accessible, along with pricing and the ability to "Select" the razor you want to purchase.

The only potential downside here is the fact that the one-sentence description for each type of blade is below the scroll line, and there's no clear indicator that it's there.

However, Dollar Shave Club has that covered with its "Compare Blades" button just under the headline.

But this raises a good point. No matter what your business, it's critical to make the most important information readily available to the visitor. In the case of mobile, making it available *before* the scroll line is a considerable bump up in the user experience department. As we'll see, it's also great for conversion.

In the case of Dollar Shave Club, notice the decision to address the blade comparison issue with a "Compare Blades" call-to-action button. The button is technically a conversion method, but it will be clicked only for visitors who don't already know what kind of blade they typically use.

You'll also notice arrows on the middle of the page. At first glance they look like a traditional carousel, but in actuality the arrows help you navigate to the blades partly visible on the left- and right-hand side of the page. This is an interesting, effective way to handle multiple product choices on one page — *once again without requiring the visitor to scroll*. But I wonder how effective it is as a UX solution. Once you tap an arrow, functionality becomes obvious, but for some users the arrow (in-and-of-itself) may not afford enough understanding to be clear without taking action.

There are other ways Dollar Shave Club could have tackled blade comparisons. For instance, they could have removed the reviews stars from below the pricing, making room for the description. But as we've discussed earlier, social proof is a big deal for Dollar Shave Club, and chances are they didn't want to lose the qualifying factor of thousands of reviews (most of them very good).

> **Holistic Side Note:** *Dollar Shave's Email UX: Although this book doesn't focus on email marketing, I want to share a handful of user experience insights based on the Dollar Shave Club. They're important because they show that the goal is the same no matter which medium you're using to connect with customers.*

Dollar Shave Club does such a good job on their email campaigns that I actually look forward to hearing from them. Plus, the company doesn't jam my inbox with too many emails, which makes the one or two I receive per month more welcome.

Here's an email I received that focused on a product I've ordered before.

Subject line:
Stop. Buttertime.

What makes the UX great:
- A nice large image that's easy to identify, even on mobile.
- A brief, clear, easy-to-read headline.
- A clear CTA button ... if I need more Shave Butter, all I have to do is click the button to get more.
- A bit of copy BELOW the headline and CTA. Why below? Because it's not as important as the image, headline and CTA.
- A second CTA, a text link, at the bottom.
- The hierarchy of this page is clear and well designed ... very solid UX!

Here's one for a product I haven't tried:

Subject line:
The search for better hair is over.

What makes the UX great:
- This email is structurally different from the previous one. Why? Because this is for a product I have not yet tried.
- I have a nice headline — along with a big RELEVANT image that pays off the headline.
- Next up is a bit of copy that also pays off the headline and the image (great continuity!). Again, this is different from the previous email example because I have not yet tried this product, so I'm probably less familiar with it.
- Now that Dollar Shave Club has given me three benefit-driven details (headline, image, copy), it's time for the CTA.
- In this example, a little more "romance" was needed before asking the email recipient to take action.
- In other words, placing the CTA right below the headline (as in the previous example) is too soon; I need more information before I can make a decision.

Unfortunately, even Dollar Shave Club's great UX can't change the fact that I don't have a lot of hair on my head. But if you click on the "Meet Your Match Button," you'll find the company has my demographic covered as well with an "I Don't Have Hair" option. When it comes to not leaving anyone out, this company pays attention to detail!

From Dollar Shave Club's desktop, to its mobile website, to its email campaigns, the company provides an excellent user experience that's also incredibly consistent. Its efforts are a brilliant example of how to effectively create a top-notch UX with a high-performing conversion strategy mixed right in.

Desktop Subpage Example #2
Here's one of Lighthouse Healing Massage Therapy's subpages. An informational page as opposed to a selling page such as that of a Dollar Shave Club subpage, it provides an easy-to-digest UX with a clean, clear page hierarchy.

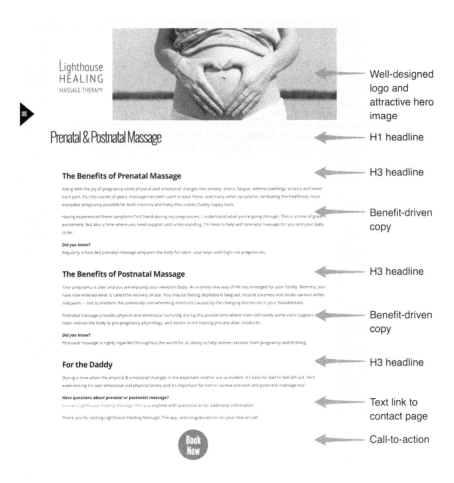

As you can see, the hierarchy of the page makes it easy to scan. If a visitor were interested in only postnatal massage, for example, the H3 helps her find it right away — but all of the major points are segmented and easily identifiable. Segmenting content into bite-sized pieces goes a long way in providing a better user experience.

And notice that we've got just ONE call-to-action here. Nice and clear. This particular client, who happens to be my wife, didn't want her call-to-action at the top or middle of the page. Why? Because as a healer, she didn't want any of her website pages to feel like a hard sell. So we placed the CTA at the bottom of the page.

But I wanted to make sure the CTA was something that was in line with the design and overall user experience of the site. Choosing a circle gave the CTA a more organic feel, as opposed to a rectangular button, yet it's still obviously a button.

Mobile Subpage Example #2

On mobile, the hierarchy of Lighthouse Healing's Prenatal and Postnatal Massage page is the same. Less of it is visible because of the smaller screen, but it's still easy to scan, thanks to the way the page is segmented with H3 headlines. In the following image, the dashes represent the scroll line ...

Prenatal & Postnatal Massage

The Benefits of Prenatal Massage

Along with the joy of pregnancy come physical and emotional changes like anxiety, stress, fatigue, edema (swelling), sciatica and lower back pain. For thousands of years, massage has been used to ease these, and many other symptoms, facilitating the healthiest, most enjoyable pregnancy possible for both mommy and baby (this makes Daddy happy too!).

Having experienced these symptoms first hand during my pregnancies, I understand what you're going through. This is a time of great excitement, but also a time where you need support and understanding. I'm here to help with prenatal massage for you and your baby to be.

Did you know?
Regularly scheduled prenatal massage prepares the body for labor, and helps with high-risk pregnancies.

The Benefits of Postnatal Massage

Your pregnancy is over and you are enjoying your newborn baby. An entirely new way of life has emerged for your family. Mommy, you have now entered what is called the *recovery* phase. You may be feeling depleted & fatigued, muscle soreness and strain, various aches and pains — not to mention the potentially overwhelming emotions caused by the changing hormones in your bloodstream.

Desktop Subpage Example #3

Next up is a subpage example from the Cuppa SEO website.

Before we dive into each of the six highlighted points in our screenshot, there's an overall UX strategy at play here (as there was on Lighthouse Healing and Dollar Shave Club) I'd like to touch on ...

Less but better.

Of notice here is that there's nothing unnecessary or flashy on this subpage. There's neither overdesign nor fancy motion graphics on the page. One of the key aspects of a solid UX is simplicity (not to be confused with under-designed). In other words, what are the nonessentials that can be removed from a subpage (or any page for that matter) that distract from the *essential*?

This is not a new concept. It can be seen clearly in the work of Jony Ive (Apple) as well as Dieter Rams, who was a designer for four decades at Braun. With design, Rams has said his goal throughout his career has been "to design functional, user-friendly products ... simple, pleasant and easy to operate." He sums it up quite well when he states "good design is as little design as possible." This is the essence of UX, making the design about the user first and foremost.

In addition, here are six ways this subpage contributes to a solid UX:

1. We see a single, easy-to-digest navigation with the hierarchy we discussed earlier — leading off with our most important tabs.
2. Our hero image is engaging (not to mention colorful), and as you'll see, it renders well on mobile, too.
3. H1 Headline: our main page headline is clear and compelling to any business that wants more relevant traffic.
4. The three short paragraphs are what I like to call "introductory copy," because they succinctly and CLEARLY answer the three "magic" questions we discussed earlier:
   a. What is it?
   b. What does it do?
   c. How does it help me (benefits)?

   Succinctness is a key point, because we want to give just enough information to answer these questions at the top of the page. Here's why …

5. It makes it possible for us to present our call-to-action ABOVE the scroll line. Which means if someone is ready to take action after reading the introductory copy, we've made it as easy as possible to do so.

   This page hierarchy creates continuity with the mobile version of the page. More importantly, it pays off a web experience we've grown accustomed to on mobile devices. In other words, well-designed mobile sites often have a call-to-action ABOVE the scroll line. What we've done at Cuppa SEO is carry this mobile strategy into desktop design. The result is an improved, more seamless user experience.

6. Below the CTA is additional info (still relevant and benefit driven) for those who need it. In this example, you can see the first line of copy is visible above the scroll line, which is nice because it makes it obvious that there's more information on the page.

Holistic Side Note: Sometimes it's not possible to get your CTA and additional copy to show above the scroll line — and that's OK. You might simply have too much introductory copy to be presented, or your subpage may not have a CTA. Just make sure you're purposefully developing the very best user experience possible on your subpages.

Mobile Subpage Example #3

Sticking with the same Cuppa SEO subpage, we see the continuity between desktop and mobile I mentioned earlier ...

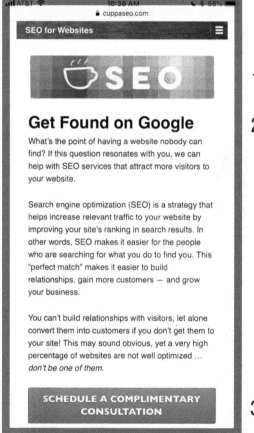

The first five UX points mentioned for the desktop version of this page hold true here, while the sixth point (having supplemental copy live above the scroll line) is a nice to have, but often difficult to achieve.

That said, there are a few mobile-centric points worth mentioning:

1. Hero image is engaging, and easy to see and understand on mobile.
2. Headline and page content are easy to read (even for those of us with older eyes), as well as clear, compelling and benefit driven.
3. A clear call-to-action button is visible without having to scroll to it.

Honoring all of the criteria we've reviewed in Chapter 7 can sometimes be a challenge — but as you can see, they're imperative components to a successful UX. Now that you know what good UX looks like, you can assess your website and honestly answer the question: How's the UX?

Since there's no one-size-fits-all answer, you need to examine what the best solutions are for your organization — and for your customers.

Again, here's what I suggest you avoid at all costs!

7. Conversion (CV)

Now that we have visitors feeling good about where they've arrived (thanks to our most excellent user experience), we need a solid conversion strategy to ensure that they know exactly what to do next.

In this chapter, we'll look at how to apply your learnings about CV from Part 1 of this book into your website. Specifically, we'll focus on:

- Website Conversion on Your Homepage
- Web Design and the Art of Conversion
- Website Conversion on Your Subpages
- The CTA Lifecycle
- Carousels, Parallax and Pop-ups

As we learned earlier, the CliffsNotes definition of conversion is: a strategy that takes a website visitor from where they are to where you want them to go.

We'll be focusing pretty heavily here on a particular part of website conversion, the Call-to-Action (CTA), which often takes the form of a button on your website.

Let's dive in with some examples ...

WEBSITE CONVERSION ON YOUR HOMEPAGE
There is no one-size-fits-all solution for website conversion, but there are some proven strategies to consider when assessing what's best for your brand, your goals and your website.

On the following pages, we'll discuss a variety of CTA strategies, and we'll also talk about the science and philosophy of CTA placement.

The Dinner Date vs. the Introduction
Let's begin with a successful strategy that includes two CTAs on the homepage. As you'll see, this strategy provides two major calls-to-action that can often satisfy a large portion of your visitor demographics.

RogerWolkoff.com
In the following example, we're using two CTAs on the homepage for Roger Wolkoff's website. Roger is a professional speaker, and he's also one of our local clients.

Here's how I sketched out the site, based on Roger's input, to ensure that solid UX and conversion strategies were brewed right in. I don't think I drank any coffee while I worked on this with Roger, although he always seemed to have a cup.

The finalized homepage looks like this:

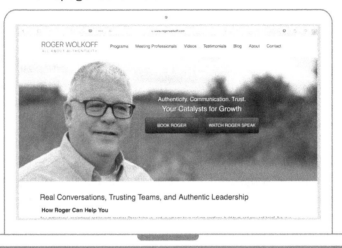

Now, let's examine our calls-to-action ...

- CTA 1 — Book Roger
  The most important call-to-action for this client, "Book Roger," is the #1 action Roger would like a potential client to take. This button is for visitors who are ready to hire Roger. Metaphorically, this potential client is ready for a first date. The person probably already knows Roger, has seen him speak, or has been referred to him. Regardless, the individual is ready to discuss booking him as a professional speaker for an event.

- CTA 2 — Watch Roger Speak
  The second call-to-action, "Watch Roger Speak," is almost as important as the first — but it serves a different purpose. This CTA is for visitors who are not yet ready for that first date. They need an introduction, "Hi, my name is Roger, and this is who I am," before committing to go out to dinner. In other words, CTA 2 is there for those who are not yet ready to commit to booking Roger but want to learn more.

On mobile, these same CTAs serve the same purpose, but they need completely different placement to remain effective. Once again, here's the mobile homepage sketch I made before we started building the site:

And here's the finalized page:

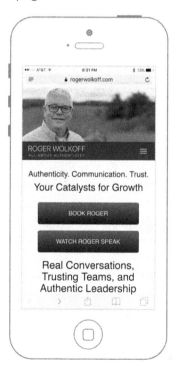

Now CTA1 and CTA2 have become buttons that sit below Roger's hero shot and tagline. Easy to spot, easy to read — and easy to understand. That's a recipe for great website conversion and an excellent UX!

As you can see from these examples, there should never be anything random about where your conversion strategy leads someone. Be crystal clear about your conversion strategy's intention. In other words, if you're that dental office we talked about earlier wanting to encourage more people to call and make an appointment, don't make the mistake of offering a free ebook as your CTA.

If you're thinking "this dinner date vs. introduction combo seems familiar," that's because we talked about it in the first part of the book when we defined conversion. Here, I wanted to show you a different, real-world example that addresses the same strategy in a different way.

EarthViewYoga.com

Lately, we've been treating this dynamic duo of "first-date" and "introduction" CTAs in a slightly different way. In addition to living on the homepage in an easy-to-find spot (more on this soon), we've also been adding the "first date" CTA right into the navigation (nav) — so it's present no matter what page you're on. Like this ...

The thought behind this is to make it as easy as possible for a website visitor to take the next step in becoming an EarthView yoga student — but we don't want to be overt, salesy or pushy about it.

Hence the placement of the CTA at the tail of the navigation. In terms of UX and conversion, we know from testing that this is typically the best spot to place this type of call to action in the navigation. It's there if I want to use it; it's not in my way if I don't. Technically, this gives us three calls-to-action, and each will need to be treated differently on mobile (always think about mobile conversion as its own entity) ...

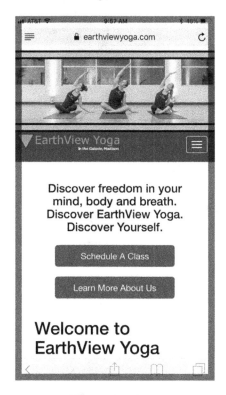

Here you can see that our solution for the on-page CTAs is pretty similar to what we did on the Roger Wolkoff site. But what happened to the third CTA? If someone is no longer on the homepage, we still want to make it easy for them to schedule a class. So, once you expand the sandwich nav you see this ...

Keeping in mind that we wanted to retain a great user experience (meaning we didn't want to become obnoxious, salesy or pushy on the mobile site), we kept the third CTA right in the navigation: same placement (at the tail of the navigation), same button color, same message ensures continuity between mobile and desktop — and once visitors see the CTA in the mobile nav, they can depend on it to always be there.

The Triple-play CTA

Before we go further, a word of caution: Three CTAs on a single page is A LOT. That said, there are circumstances where it might be necessary for your brand — but be certain it's really necessary before slapping three CTAs on the page. When it is necessary, we need to take the user experience into account as well as to support a solid conversion strategy that helps convert, not confuse. For example ...

RosyCheeksandCo.com

With Rosy Cheeks, we're looking at three different calls-to-action on the homepage. This is an interesting example, because Rosy Cheeks didn't have a photography budget, and the images they did have were small and pixelated. It was a definite challenge to create a homepage without any hi-res images, but it quickly turned into an opportunity to be creative about how we could use their calls-to-action as a big part of the design element.

Dancewear, Ballroom and Gymnastics are all clickable buttons that lead to their respective product pages. And since the CTAs are actually the homepage design, the overall UX is very good, as you don't have to think about what to do next. If you're not ready to click on a CTA, there's a bit of copy peeking at the bottom of the page to let you know there's more to read — if you're interested.

On mobile, you'll see we treated the homepage quite differently to ensure the very best UX for the visitor. Could you imagine if we had used the desktop Dancewear, Ballroom and Gymnastics imagery on an iPhone? It would be tough to read and tough to see what was in the imagery — making it highly tempting for visitors to hit the back button to get off the site!

Instead, we went with the Rosy Cheeks logo at the top of the mobile homepage, and we altered the look of the CTAs for an easy-to-digest experience ...

iMerge Consulting

Another triple CTA homepage example is iMerge. During the web design prep process, the client actually wanted more than three CTAs so visitors would see everything offered as soon as they got to the homepage (no scrolling). In case you missed it earlier, that can lead a website to look like the following ...

For iMerge, we were able to pare down the CTAs to three (which accounts for about 80% of their business).

iMerge is an international firm, and one of the company's goals is to guide customers through the world of information governance. We chose a compass, which turned out to be an ideal and pervasive theme for the site. For the homepage, we created custom art that integrates their international reach with an aesthetic that plays right into the compass theme — with the CTAs playing a prominent role in the design.

We took it one step further and made the CTAs interactive when you hover over them ...

iMerge is an excellent example of using design to ensure solid UX and conversion strategies — even when there are multiple CTAs. That said, it's best in most cases to keep your CTAs to a maximum of three. Adding more can really damage the user experience (not to mention your website conversion percentage).

On mobile, we once again took a more simplified strategy where all three CTAs live above the scroll line ...

With mobile, it's important to ensure that your UX and conversion strategies outweigh your designer's need to be creative. In other words, big CTAs that don't all fit above the scroll line are often a bad choice (even if they look pretty). And if you have a lot of them, you're asking visitors to scroll, and scroll, and scroll to *maybe* find what they want.

The Solo CTA

They say one is a lonely number ... but it's also a very *effective* number when it's a call-to-action.

Before we begin, it's important to note that a single CTA is not the right solution for every brand. But when it is, it provides an uncluttered, super-easy-to-digest next step for a visitor to take.

Let's take a look at three different types of single CTAs: 1) the strong product/service CTA, 2) the informational CTA, 3) and the soft sell CTA (not to be confused with the '80s band *Soft Cell*).

The Strong Product/Service CTA

Talarczyk Land Surveys, a business that focuses on one major service — land surveys — provides a great example of a brand that benefits from the single CTA solution. Why? Their main goal, by a long shot, is to have potential clients call them.

Much like our EarthView Yoga example from earlier in this section, we've placed Talarczyk's CTA right in their navigation; it's an easy-to-find spot that's present on every page of the site. We did this for two reasons:

1. We wanted to make sure it was super-easy for a visitor to get in touch no matter where they were on the site. Placement, color and size of this CTA accomplishes the goal nicely.

2. We wanted to keep the hero image on the homepage as clean and engaging as possible without being "salesy." Could we have placed a CTA on the hero shot? Sure. In fact, we tried many iterations, and they all diminished the overall user experience of the homepage, making it more complex, harder to digest, and reducing aesthetic impact (plus the cows didn't like it). So, we got rid of it.

Same deal on mobile. Making it easy for someone to get in touch is paramount, and we also wanted to keep continuity with the aesthetic of the desktop homepage. In this case, we were able to keep the hero image, as it still looks good on mobile — and as you've seen, that's not always easy to achieve.

Once again, we've created a mobile hierarchy where the CTA lives above the scroll line, making it super easy for someone with a smartphone to place the call.

As with EarthView Yoga, we wanted to retain a great user experience on mobile, yet ensure that it was easy for someone to call Talarczyk from any page. So we went with the same solution here, keeping the CTA in the sandwich navigation: same placement (at the tail of the navigation) and same message to ensure continuity between mobile and desktop. We chose not to use a green button background, as the design of the mobile navigation looked great as is with a gradation from blue to green.

An important element of CTAs like these on mobile is that when visitors see it once, they know exactly where to go and what to do when they're ready to engage — without being bombarded with a salesy, pushy CTA.

The Informational CTA

Little White Fence is a wonderful small business. It's run by three sisters who decided to turn their family farm into an enterprise that would help revitalize their community. The first phase of their business plan was to open a unique shop that offered items such as distressed furniture, antiques and one-of-a-kind handmade goods.

As we went through the web design prep process, we identified the client's #1 goal: to make sure potential visitors knew how to get to the farm (they are near the Iron Mountain area of northern Wisconsin, about as off the beaten path as you can get). So, their CTA is *Get Directions* ...

We used the same placement as the Talarczyk CTA but with a different goal. Notice that here we used the same color for the CTA as the barn (rusty red), honoring the color palette of the page. The CTA also contrasts beautifully with the blue sky. (Color plays a big part in making CTAs easy to find).

On mobile, we decided to go with the text logo for the hero image, as it played right into the distressed furniture and antiques sold at Little White Fence. The large text also made a stronger impact than if we had shrunk the barn to smartphone size. And it's why the CTA didn't work well above the scroll line: There wasn't enough room for introductory copy AND the CTA button.

We still needed to create a CTA in a prominent place so potential customers could find the shop, but we didn't want it below the scroll line, so once again we leaned on the sandwich navigation ...

And we kept the same color and placement to ensure continuity with the desktop CTA (we love continuity, and so should you), which made it easy for a website visitor to get directions.

The "Soft Sell" CTA

If you're lucky enough to live in the Madison, Wisconsin, area, you can book a massage with one of the greatest healers around ... my wife, Kara, the owner of Lighthouse Healing Massage Therapy. Although I'm extremely partial, I'm not kidding about her talents.

When I showed her the proposed CTA placement on her new website, she looked at me and said ... "NO."

I wanted the CTA in a prominent place to make it as easy as possible for someone to book an appointment. But Kara made a compelling point: She is a healer, and she doesn't want even the slightest hint of someone needing her services to feel as if they are being "sold" in any way, shape or form.

This brings us back to a critical point of online marketing: **You've always got to be true to who you are** as a brand (which quite often mirrors your personal values). We never want to sacrifice a brand's truth or identity for the sake of conversion (or anything else for that matter).

So after promptly thanking my lovely wife for the extra work to find a new solution, I got right to it — because there's always a solution.

As you can see from the desktop homepage, there is no CTA above the scroll line ...

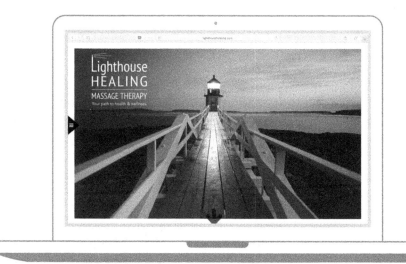

... just an engaging image and tagline, "Lighthouse Healing Massage Therapy — your path to health and wellness." Here's how we solved the CTA challenge my wife presented to us.

Solution #1
Scrolling down to the bottom of the page, we find our CTA ...

The goal here was to make this CTA easy-to-spot, organic, and totally in alignment with the Lighthouse Healing brand. Yes, it's at the bottom of the page instead of the top — and it's true that this solution is not typical — but it was the best solution for this particular client.

Solution #2
But we weren't done yet ... we needed to make sure that a visitor could EASILY book an appointment from *anywhere* on the site (it's the same goal we had for EarthView Yoga's "Take a Class" CTA, or Little White Fence's "Get Directions" CTA).

Since we decided to employ a sandwich navigation on the desktop version of the site, we placed the "Schedule an Appointment" tab in a prominent place, just below the Services tab ...

When we launched the site, I looked at these CTA solutions as a test, which is what I like to do with ALL CTAs. I was fully prepared to test a change, if necessary, but on average, Kara books 4-8 new clients a month (just from online search), which is all she can handle. So we decided to leave the CTAs alone because they're working well.

On the mobile site, we took a similar approach, removing the CTA from above the scroll line ...

and placing it at the bottom of the page ...

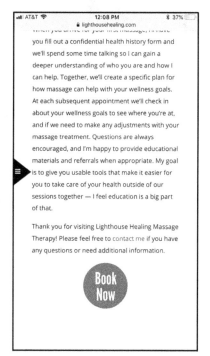

And, as with our other examples, it's in a prominent place in the sandwich navigation, just after all of the services, so it's easy to access no matter where you are on the site.

Holistic Side Note: Horizontal awesomeness! You probably noticed that the mobile Lighthouse Healing homepage switched out the hero image for the company logo. We did this because the hero image looked too small on a smartphone. Then one of our designers (Jared) suggested trying the hero shot in landscape mode, and it looked great! This is an excellent example of going BEYOND simple responsive design, where a page is more than mobile friendly — and is actually designed for the best user experience. In this case, the user experience changes from portrait mode to landscape mode (logo-only in landscape didn't look right), and we've designed accordingly ...

Back to our regularly scheduled program on conversion ... it's important to note that the Lighthouse Healing homepage CTA leads us to some major questions:

1. Why, dear author, is it important to place our CTAs in the spots you're suggesting?

2. What if I don't want my CTA in one of these spots (as was the case with Lighthouse healing)? Is there a solution? And if so, please explain.

These questions lead us to ...

WEB DESIGN AND THE ART OF CONVERSION
Let's start off with question #1: Why, dear author, is it important to place our CTAs in the spots you're suggesting?

Through tons and tons of research with actual people, user experience and conversion experts have determined some pretty interesting lessons (at least I think they're interesting). One is that on a laptop or desktop computer, there are "hot spots" to which the human eye is typically drawn. Let's take a look at these hot spots, which make up what I like to call the "F-Zone."

The "F-zone"
The following screen shot identifies the hot spots of a web page — in other

words, areas that naturally attract the human eye. These are areas we want to seriously consider as spots for our important information — in this case, the call-to-action.

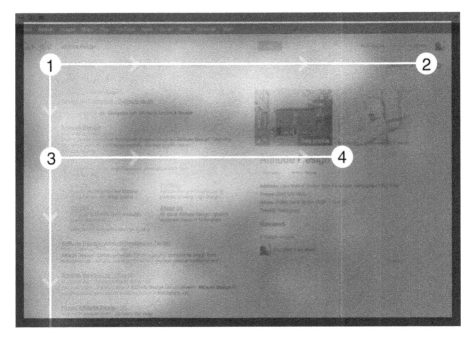

- Area 1–2 is often reserved for a website's navigation, which can include a call-to-action, as we've already seen with EarthView Yoga and Little White Fence.

- Area 3–4 is a great place for CTAs, as they sit right in the pocket of the F-Zone. We saw this used extremely well on the Roger Wolkoff and Dollar Shave Club sites.

- Area 1–3, going all the way to the bottom of the screen is also a powerful spot for CTAs and can sometimes be used effectively for navigation (as we saw in the J. Crew example in the UX section of the book).

Here's a nice example of Area 1–3 being used for CTAs. We worked on this site a few years ago and ran our own UX tests to confirm (or possibly debunk) how well this hot zone worked for a local chain of dentists' offices, First Choice Dental:

Here, we were able to incorporate the CTAs right into a hotspot, and right into the design of the page (an important element in the success or failure of a CTA). It tested well, and we've been using this solution ever since!

Because of its innate power to attract the human eye, the F-Zone is something you'll want to consider when planning your website conversion. But we still have a second question to address.

Question #2: What if, as was the case with Lighthouse Healing, you don't want your CTA in the F-Zone? OR what if it simply doesn't fit with your brand or design to place CTAs in the F-Zone?" This leads us to ...

The Alternative to the F-zone

The answer to question #2 became crystal clear to me when I saw the following image in one of my design books, *100 Ideas That Changed Graphic Design.*

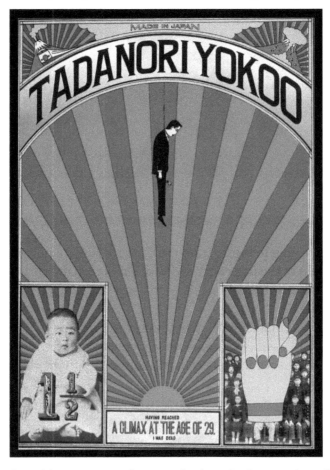

What's the first thing you see when you look at the image above? I'll bet it's one of five things:

1. The Tadanori Yokoo headline
2. The man displayed over the rays (Yes, he's being hung ... ewww.)
3. The baby in the lower left corner
4. Or the hand in the lower right
5. OK, so you probably also noticed the iconic rays in the background.

This piece of art was created by graphic designer Tadanori Yokoo in 1965.

Although this piece, and much of Tadanori's work, is known for the layering of red rays into culturally charged art, it's also an excellent example of how graphic design can control the eye of the viewer.

How Tadanori's Art Relates to Conversion on Your Website
We just saw that the F-Zone is a tested, proven strategy for solid conversion. Knowing where the eye gravitates to on a web page is a great insight, but just because something is proven and tested doesn't mean it's your only option — or the BEST option for your website/brand.

Knowing where the eye is naturally drawn is one thing, but what if I want to manipulate where the eye is drawn?

What Tadanori's art shows us ...
... is that through the use of aesthetic, we can break the rules. Instead of depending on the eyes' natural tendencies, we can direct they eyes to where we want them to go through the use of design and color — while still keeping the level of conversion high and ensuring an excellent user experience.

Here's an example of how Tadanori's image can be translated into a desktop homepage, with all of the important elements appearing above the fold:

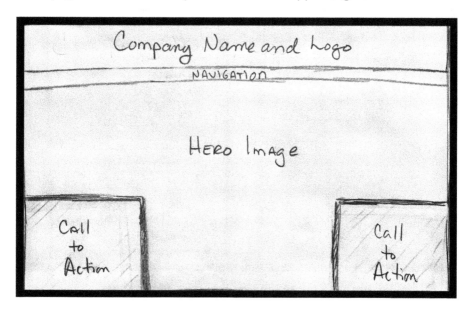

As you can see, the bottom right element is completely out of the F-Zone, but is easy to spot and still catches the eye. Of course, the bottom left element is in the F-Zone. There's no denying that BOTH of these calls-to-action immediately catch the eye — and this is only a black and white sketch! Imagine what can be done with color and imagery.

The point here is that we don't always need to blindly follow "protocol" and place CTAs where they "belong." There's always a solution to make things work within your brand's vision as long as you're willing to think creatively and unconventionally, and use design to support your UX and conversion strategies.

Here's an example of how Tadanori's art can be further manipulated to be effective on a mobile device. Because the F-Zone doesn't come into play on mobile as it does on a desktop, there's a different set of successful strategies we like to follow (we've already discussed many of them). The sketch on the left is a Tadanori-centric solution; the sketch on the right offers a more traditional solution for solid conversion. The modified design still works, and it actually fits quite nicely into the strategies we've developed for conversion on mobile — in this case with two clear calls-to-action visible without the need to scroll.

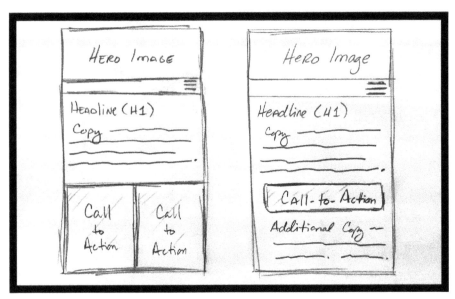

Solutions like these are not right for everybody, and I'm not suggesting you abandon the F-Zone for a Tadanori-inspired conversion strategy. But you'll have to admit that it looks great, and it's a solid solution for SOME brands.

A Real-World Example

Here's the current iteration of Cuppa SEO's homepage, with both CTAs living outside the F-Zone. This started off as a simple test to see how the alternative F-Zone could perform in the real world.

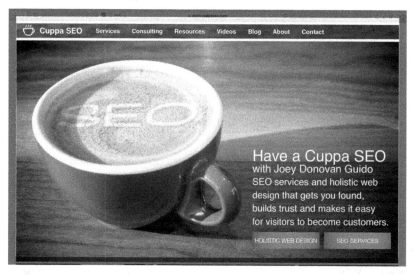

Originally, I had tried many different CTA buttons in the F-Zone. Somewhere in this area ...

None of my trial CTAs were very successful. I tired different colors and different messages, and still this veritable "hot spot" left me feeling cold (and somehow a little sad).

Over the years, I've realized that our services aren't something a visitor dives into from a homepage CTA. In other words, potential clients like to peruse the site a bit and then get in touch. But that didn't mean I was satisfied with poorly performing CTAs!

So I stopped thinking about the F-Zone and started thinking about what made sense.

- A visitor arrives on the site (yay!)
- He (hopefully) engages with the warm colors, the coffee and the humanness of the page.
- He reads the (intentionally) sparse copy, which is clear and to the point.

Well, I asked myself, what about that little bit of real estate just below the copy? That's where my eye naturally seems to go to next — even without a CTA there — because I just read the copy, which naturally draws my eye down. What if I place the CTAs there and use a contrasting (yet still complementary) red button to also draw the eye there?

It worked. Employing the Tadanori philosophy gave my homepage conversion an immediate boost, somewhere between two and three times what it was previously.

WEBSITE CONVERSION ON YOUR SUBPAGES
Next up, let's take a look at a couple of subpage CTAs on desktop and mobile. First is Dollar Shave Club, which of course is an online retail shop. So the idea is to sell stuff, right? Dollar Shave Club makes it easy ...

We saw earlier that Dollar Shave Club provides an excellent UX, which greatly supports the website conversion on its site. For instance, as soon as we get to the Blades page, we know where we are, what our choices are and what to do next. Three crystal-clear calls-to-action make it easy to choose the right blade.

And although there's a line of copy followed by some bullet points below the scroll line, they're unobtrusive. So if I'm ready to buy (the first date) I can just click SELECT. If I need a little more information (the introduction), I can easily read the content below the CTA — which completely supports the CTA and helps visitors take the next step to becoming a customer.

Honestly, when I first looked at this page, I was curious as to how Dollar Shave Club could pull off equally impressive UX and conversion on mobile. But the company did a pretty good job ...

Dollar Shave Club set up its mobile conversion in a very clever way.

To begin, ALL THREE blades are visible, even on a mobile device. The middle blade lines up with the CTA below it — accompanied by some uncluttered info: price and an excellent star rating. Thanks to the solid UX, there's no distraction, and the eye easily focuses on the CTA.

BUT, if this is not the blade for me, I can see blades that are for thinner and thicker beards, respectively, without having to scroll or tap on anything (again, excellent UX that supports conversion). If I click on one of the arrows below the other two razors, the razor I'm interested in moves to the center along with that razor's details and SELECT button.

This is a beautiful way to present information so the visitor sees multiple options WITHOUT being overwhelmed. New information is presented only when called for by the user, creating a streamlined look that makes it easy for visitors to buy.

Now, let's move on to a couple of services-driven subpages on CuppaSEO.com.

Our first example is our Web Design page, which is clean, uncluttered and easy to digest.

Notice the three major elements on the page:
1. Hero image: occupies upper-left corner of the F-Zone
2. Page headline: "The Benefits of Holistic Web Design"
3. On-page CTA button: "Contact Us About Web Design"

The CTA is placed high on the page because of the influence of smartphones. CTAs used to live primarily at the bottom of a page as a text link (although sometimes closer to the top of the page). But the influx of mobile devices changed that.

Well-designed mobile websites began presenting clear CTA buttons above the scroll line, and we consumers ate it up like ice cream on a hot day. As mobile-device users, our minds started to expect these CTAs to be present on mobile — which makes sense, because these CTAs provide a good UX (in addition to being good for conversion).

And because our brains began to expect CTAs on mobile, it was a natural progression to fulfill this same expectation on desktop. That's why you see our CTA so high on the page.

The placement of this CTA is very deliberate.

First, we needed to make sure enough information was presented ABOVE the CTA to ensure that visitors who needed *a little bit of information* before taking action got what they wanted. To accomplish this, we went to our go-to questions about our web-design services:

1. What is it?
2. What does it do?
3. How does it help me?

Completely answering all of these questions before the call-to-action would mean that the CTA would sit at the bottom of the page, ruining our goal to make the desktop conversion experience similar to mobile. But taking a similar approach as Dollar Shave Club, we placed just enough information above the CTA to clearly define the service — and a whole lot more below it for visitors who needed more details to make a decision.

Consider what happens when we look at the mobile version of the Web Design page, where ...

... you'll immediately notice that you don't see the CTA!

This is why we never call anything a "best practice," because there are exceptions. This is one of them. Let me explain.

The issue here was twofold:

- To move the CTA higher on the page so it would show above the fold on mobile, we would have had to remove some of the defining copy from the top of the page. If this were the only issue, it would have been solvable.

- When the CTA sat higher on the page, it was too close to the hero image on the desktop version, breaking the balance of the page: The two elements fought with each other for attention. Although it looked great on mobile, I couldn't risk a desktop visitor having a bad user experience, so we placed the CTA a little lower on the page. Now it looked great on desktop, but a visitor would have to scroll about two inches on a mobile phone to see the CTA. This solution was acceptable to me, because the CTA was still pretty close to the top of the mobile page, and it sat in the perfect spot on the desktop view.

This issue also could have been solved by creating widgets for this subpage. We could have created different button placements for desktop and mobile sites within these widgets, as you saw us do in the homepage examples earlier. But I wanted to avoid this type of solution, because it could get messy if we wanted to update our content as it would have required changes in TWO places instead of in one place.

Another solution could have been to forgo the upper left-hand corner placement of the hero image, but because that was designed to work seamlessly with some of our social media efforts, it was too sizeable a compromise. Essentially, hero image size and placement worked well on social media, because when we dropped a link to the web design page in our social post, the image *automatically populated* in the post AND *linked directly to our web design page* — which was a big win for higher conversion. More on this later in the social media section.

That being said, here's an example of another Cuppa SEO subpage that employs a different design ...

As with the Web Design page, the CTA button sits above the scroll line. And because of the different design of the hero image, it does the same on mobile …

Just remember, there's always an answer, but you might have to approach things differently in order to find it.

THE CTA LIFECYCLE

Thus far in our discussion on conversion, we've focused our attention on strategy, theory and implementation of CTAs on your website's homepage and subpages. Now it's time for a broader look at the CTA so we can get an idea of its complete lifecycle. In this section we'll take a look at:

- Defining your CTAs
- Where CTAs lead
- Subpage/Squeeze page criteria
- The thank you page
- Tracking & testing

Defining Your CTAs

Before you implement your CTAs, you've got to determine exactly what they are. We talked about this earlier in the book, but it's worth repeating, because clearly understanding the most important thing(s) you want a visitor to do next is a critical part of your business' success.

Notice how I said *the most important thing*, not what you or someone on your team wants most. If someone influential at your company wants, more than anything, to have the company's free ebook downloaded by everyone who visits the site, it's important not to cave and just say yes. How will these ebook downloads affect the business, if at all? Will it drive sales? Further engagement? Reputation improvement? Stroking someone's ego?

Before the ebook is even proposed or seriously considered, your team has to decide what your top goals are — as a brand. And once your goals are clearly defined, then you can define the top 1–3 things you want people to do when they get to your website. Here are just a few options ...

- Call
- Email
- Fill out a form
- Buy
- Schedule an appointment
- Watch an informational video
- Download an ebook or infographic

This strategy ensures that your CTAs are in alignment with your goals, making it more probable that you'll succeed in accomplishing those goals.

Where CTAs Lead to: Subpages and Squeeze Pages

Once goals and CTAs are defined and in perfect alignment, it's time to think about where these CTAs lead to. CTAs typically lead to a subpage (like your contact page or a product page), or to a specific squeeze page/landing page.

The purpose of a squeeze page is to directly fulfill the expectation set up by the CTA. They're a little different from a subpage (like a services page) because they can typically be accessed only by clicking on the CTA.

Squeeze pages can be for a product, service, special deal or promotion — pretty much anything you want. They're super helpful when running Adwords campaigns, social media promotions, or for anytime you want to create a clean, clear, succinct page that focuses on making it easy for a website visitor to take the next step in obtaining a product or service.

Let's take a look at a few examples of where CTAs lead.

On the Cuppa SEO website, some of our CTAs lead directly to the Contact page. The path looks like this …

A visitor lands on our Web Design page …

… clicks on the CTA, and is directed to the Contact page …

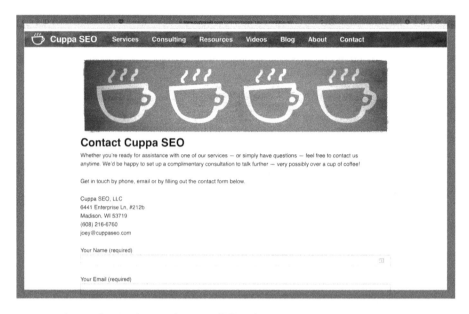

Let's review what's above the scroll line here:

- In this distraction-free environment, visitors are presented with the opportunity to get in touch via phone, email or by filling out a SIMPLE form. I've made it easy for them to accomplish the task they set out to do when they clicked on my call-to-action.

- A simple, engaging image sits at the top of the page. We wanted some visual interest without distracting visitors from accomplishing what we want them to do — connect with us!

- Introductory copy is very brief. Remember: In this case, the visitor came from one of our services pages — which contains lots of pertinent info — and decided to click on the call-to-action: "Contact Us About Web Design." We don't need to give that person more info about web design here; we need to make it as easy as possible for visitors to do what they're expecting to do ... contact Cuppa SEO.

- Because every person is different, we want to make it as easy as possible for a visitor to get in touch in a way that's most comfortable. It's why we present our phone number, email and contact form — all above the scroll line (on a 13" MacBook Pro).

Some people don't like to fill out forms, because they somehow wind up on email and newsletter lists (remember the dark side of conversion we talked about?). Our phone number and email gives them options (and makes us appear approachable, too).

- It's imperative that at least a couple of the form fields appear above the scroll line. It's important for both UX and conversion, because the visitor doesn't have to wonder, "Is there a form on this page?" Whether it's conscious or subconscious, we don't want the visitor to think it — so avoid forms buried below the fold whenever possible.

Here's what the entire form looks like ...

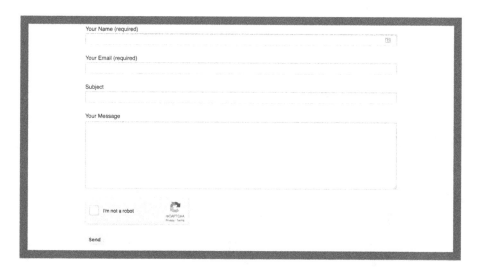

Keeping the number of fields to a minimum helps increase conversion. The less we ask of visitors, the easier it is for them to take the next step. That said, make sure you're getting the initial information you need — and save the rest to acquire in the follow up!

The reCATPTCHA form at the bottom is an important component for a couple of reasons:
- It provides a much better UX for the user to simply click a box as opposed to entering letters and numbers to prove they're not a robot.

- It provides a much better UX for YOU when you're not getting a ton of spam from bots!

Moving on to a squeeze page example, here's what our Adwords page looks like ...

And here's the squeeze page it leads to ...

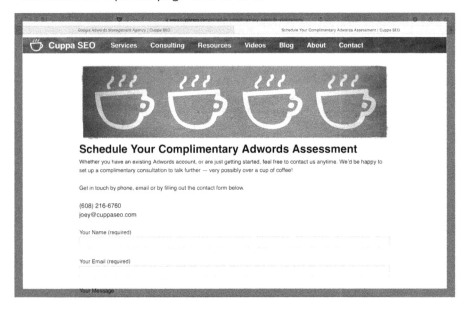

Here's the same squeeze page on mobile ...

Now, keep in mind that in both of these examples, a visitor is brought to the Contact or squeeze page from an actual Cuppa SEO web page — which means the person had at least a one-page introduction to who we are and what we do BEFORE getting to the Contact or squeeze page.

That's one of the reasons these pages are so sparse: It's not the visitor's first introduction to Cuppa SEO. If it were, I would consider including more content on these pages and having them be more visually stimulating. Let's look at a couple of examples of this.

Where CTAs Lead from: Adwords or Social Media

When someone engages with a CTA in a Google Adword listing or from a social media post, the strategy shifts a bit, because this IS potentially their first interaction on our website. When that's the case, we need to pay off our CTA and engage with the visitor differently.

In one of our Adwords campaigns with Widen, an international software company, we drive people from an Adwords ad directly to this squeeze page ...

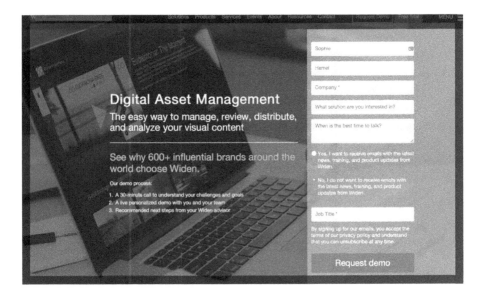

As you can see, we've got a little bit of content on the left, answering these questions: 1) What is it?; 2) What does it do?; 3) How can it help me from a high level? (in other words, not a lot of detail).

Our form is smack dab on the right of the page — above the fold — making it easy to find and fill out without additional effort on the visitor's part. This is a good UX and good for conversion.

Holistic Side Note: With the advent of GDPR (General Data Protection Regulation), it will become more and more commonplace for you to see content similar to what's above the "Request demo" button on the Widen form, which reads:

- *Yes, I want to receive emails with the latest news, training, and product updates from Widen.*

- *No, I do not want to receive emails with the latest news, training, and product updates from Widen.*

That's all we intend to cover about GDPR in this book, but if you're not familiar with it, ask your web developer for help to make sure your site is compliant.

This squeeze page is set up a little differently ...

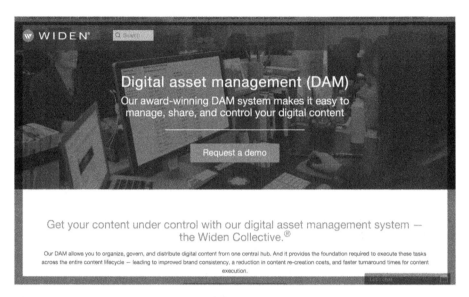

This one is set up more like a traditional subpage, again with a minimal amount of information above the scroll line, along with another CTA button that, when clicked, automatically takes you to the form at the bottom of the page (basic anchor text technique).

In both of these cases, the squeeze page offers minimal information above the scroll, and it is more visually engaging than the Cuppa SEO examples we saw earlier. And if you're a visitor who's ready to "Request a Demo," that's all you need.

But what if your need more info?

Remember, this is the visitor's first exposure to the Widen website, and in addition to the slightly elevated visual engagement, we want to have more product information for those who need it. All of this sits below the scroll line ...

Just below the scroll line is a well-produced, SHORT video that offers more information about Widen's product. And as you can see, there is content just below the video that helps the visitor learn more about the product.

At the bottom of the page, the CTA "Request a Demo" repeats. If someone is ready to take the next step, we've made it easy. It's important to have the CTA at the bottom of the page identical to what was at the top. If it's not, the visitor might get confused by mixed messaging. If you have two messages at the top — "Watch Our Video" and "Request a Demo" — it's not only fine, but it's a good idea to repeat both of them at the bottom of the page, too. But be consistent!

As we near the end of the conversion section, I want to make sure I reiterate the fact that you've got to test all of this out yourself — on your website — to see what works best with YOUR visitors. There's more than one way to successfully create a squeeze page, so you'll just have to test, test, test. Be sure to alter only one thing at a time, or you won't know what helped or hurt the page!

The Thank You Page

Once someone submits a form, what happens next? Depending on how you have your website set up, there might be a little on-page message that says "Message Sent," like this ...

> Your message was sent successfully. Thanks.

Or, you could add a Thank You page to automatically trigger when someone fills out one of your forms. Here's what ours looks like (it's intentionally streamlined, basic and to the point) ...

Edit Page · Cuppa SEO — WordPress   Thank You! | Cuppa SEO   Search Engine Optimization Services | Cuppa SEO

Cuppa SEO   Services   Consulting   Resources   Videos   Blog   About   Contact

Thank you for contacting Cuppa SEO!
We'll be in touch soon ...

Cuppa SEO, LLC, 6441 Enterprise Ln, #212b, Madison, WI 53719 • (608) 216-6760

The Thank You page is worth considering for at least two reasons:

1. When the Thank You page is triggered, it's obvious to your website visitors that their completed form has been successfully submitted.

2. It's one of the easiest ways to track how your form is converting in Google Analytics. Although we won't be covering this in-depth here, just know that it's possible to set the Thank You page as a goal (sometimes referred to as an event) with Google. This way, you'll have accurate insights as to how well a form is working — and with insights comes the ability to make educated changes that can be tested.

Testing
This is a test, this is only a test ...

When you think about it, all of life is a test. We try something, and it either works, kind of works, or stinks. It's the same with your online marketing, which is why you've heard me refer to testing many times throughout this book — and with good reason. The road doesn't end once our CTAs are decided upon and live on our website. We need to know what's happening with them so we can make improvements (if necessary) and leave them alone (when they're working).

In both instances, hard data on the success or failure of a CTA is critical to long-term success, and it can also be used as undeniable proof that something's working (which is why we shouldn't change it), or that something's not working (which is why we need to test something new ASAP, no matter how much someone may love 18 CTAs on a single page) ...

I could write an entire book on the subject of testing, but my knowledge of testing is not as vast as that of Chris Goward, author of *You Should Test That!* So if you want to go beyond the basic principles of testing as presented in this book, check out Chris' book — and be amazed.

What I DO want to cover here is the critical concept of testing only one thing at a time. Whether it's your homepage, subpage, squeeze page — it doesn't matter. The only way to get accurate data is to test one element of the page at a time.

In other words, you conduct what's called a *controlled test*. The reason might not be apparent at first, but if you're testing multiple items (color, CTA language, graphics, content, etc.) on a single page — how will you know what change (or changes) produced the positive or negative results you're seeing?

If it's not clear what caused your conversion rate to double, because you made so many changes to a page at one time, how can you replicate that successful strategy on other pages? If it's not clear what caused your conversion rate to plummet, same deal: You don't know exactly what to avoid going forward.

With a controlled test, you can clearly see if a conversion strategy is helping or hurting.

A/B Testing
You can do controlled testing yourself, in-house, by adding a solid A/B testing plugin or application to your website.

A/B testing is also referred to as "split testing," and it's a way to test two different versions of the same web page to see which performs better. It works like this: Two web page options are presented to visitors, option A and option B. They are identical except for ONE element, and they get equal exposure: For every 100 visitors, 50 see option A, and 50 see option B.

Before you start the test, make sure there have been **NO** changes to the page you're planning on testing for **at least the last three months.** You want this page to remain untouched for this amount of time, because you need a solid baseline of metrics from the old page before you can test the new one. In other words, I need to know what my conversion rate is for my existing page — exactly as it is — so I can compare it to the conversion rate of the test page.

How long the test lasts will depend on your traffic volume. If you get 100 hits a day, a month-long test will give you about 3,000 test participants (some will be repeat visitors). That's a pretty good amount to base a test on. On the other hand, if you have 10–20 hits a day, you might need to run the test longer to achieve the volume you need to make an educated decision.

Holistic Side Note: If you have a WordPress site, there are many A/B testing plugins you can use. Some of these are free, but that doesn't always mean they're good. Look for a plugin that has a number of positive reviews as well as frequent updates. One of the best I have found is Nelio A/B testing, which provides a lot of easy-to-digest analytics. If you don't use WordPress, the process may be a bit more involved, but it's still doable.

CAROUSELS, PARALLAX AND POP-UPS
We talked earlier (UX section, Part 2) about the downside of carousels, parallax websites and pop-ups as they pertain to the user experience. Let's look at why these strategies are bad for website conversion and why you should avoid them.

Carousels/Slideshows
As we discussed earlier, carousels/slideshows are a commonplace strategy for sharing more information through a series of sliding imagery/offers on a homepage. We've all seen them. Each slide sits front and center for a few seconds, and then it's gone.

Avoid this strategy on your website; it's bad for conversion.

We already know that website conversion is a strategy that takes a website visitor from where they are, to where you want them to go. Carousels offer too many options for where we want to lead people, challenging them to think. And although thinking is usually a good thing, we want to avoid unnecessary brain work on our website, because it can easily damage the user experience. And when the user experience is damaged, conversion can often be a casualty.

To avoid bombarding visitors with offers, you can ask yourself one simple question:

What are the top one or two things we want a website visitor to do? There's not always an easy answer, especially if you sell a lot of products or services. If this is the case for your business, it's good to employ the 80/20 rule. What 20% of your products or services account for 80% of your business? if you've got a lot of services/products, then identify the top performing product or services **categories**, instead.

Write them down.

Your goal: Pare down your top products/services to 2 or 3, and then create a strategy to present them on your homepage in a way that *avoids slideshows*.

Parallax
As touched upon earlier, a parallax website is a site that is often referred to as a "scrolling website." It's typically a single page, or just a handful of pages, with the homepage containing a TON of information.

These sites can be effective if you are selling a specific product such as a book, as the top CTA would be to buy the book, and all supporting info would be about ... the book. Parallax sites can also be effective if they are designed to tell a clear, compelling story as you scroll down the page. However, this is VERY difficult to do; I've seen it effectively executed only once or twice, and poorly executed hundreds of times.

Because a parallax website can give you the feeling of parachuting out of an airplane, it already has a built-in poor UX. And once you have a poor UX, you've damaged your credibility, making it harder for your site visitor to trust you (hence lowering conversion). On top of that, the plethora of information you're typically asked to digest — on one single parallax page — can be mind-numbing, not to mention confusing and off-putting.

Does this sound like a good environment to present a CTA? You're right, it's not.

If you simply MUST have a parallax site (for your own relevant reasons), I suggest making sure all pertinent information is presented above the scroll line — along with any CTAs you want to present. Below the scroll line can be more details to support what you've presented at the top of the page. But if you expect someone to forage through a heap of imagery, buttons and content to decipher what you're trying to tell them, you're asking for trouble. For most businesses and organizations, there are far better choices that provide a remarkably better user experience.

Pop-ups

This web experience has been interrupted by this pop-up ... just kidding, I wouldn't do that to you, dear reader. But isn't that exactly how you feel when a pop-up disrupts what you're trying to do on a website?

We've already talked about how pop-ups are poor for UX, but let's touch upon a few reasons why they're bad for conversion (of course, UX and conversion are always interrelated).

1. If the offer in your pop-up is so important, *why isn't it one of the calls-to-action on your homepage?* OK, yes, a pop-up attracts attention, but so does a barking dog — and nobody likes to be barked at. A little nuance, a little romance from a well-designed web page that includes your most important CTAs is much more likely to get you that first date we talked about.

2. Small-picture CTAs can overshadow big-picture CTAs. For example, let's revisit my experience when looking to purchase yoga gear for my wife. EVERY site I visited had a pop-up with the same message ... "Save 10% by signing up for our email list."

What's more important: the email list or making a sale? Sure, feel free to make me aware of the discount. That's great. But don't hold the discount hostage unless I give you my personal info. If I make a purchase, couldn't you then ask me if I want future special offers, news and discounts? After I've checked out and become a paying customer? Why do you have to ask me within the first three seconds I show up on your site — especially when your #1 conversion goal is to make a sale? In this case, these yoga sites were keeping up with the Joneses, but didn't realize the Joneses got it wrong.

At the end of the day, a pop-up is like any other strategy on your website ... it needs to be thought through carefully to ensure that it has the potential to accomplish your major goals — make a sale, schedule a consultation, etc. If it's not in direct alignment with your major goals, then get rid of it, or figure out a way to include it as a secondary goal that's a good UX (as we did with the yoga pants example above when we added the email signup to the end of the experience).

Even if it is in alignment with your major goals, the question remains: Is this pop-up the best way to communicate with my visitor? If it is (it's probably not), when exactly is the best time to present it so it's a good UX rather than a roadblock to building a relationship?

Remember, distraction is bad. It can reduce sales, and adds to the non-essential "noise" we're bombarded with every day. This makes the UX gods — and your website visitors — feel like crying, so get rid of any and all distraction!

PART 3: YOUR BLOG

Once your website has been addressed for SEO, UX and conversion, the next step is to learn how to apply these strategies to your blog.

8. Welcome to the World of Blogging

Now that your website is all gussied up with SEO, UX and CV, blogging is the next natural step in your online marketing process.

Why? Because blogging needs to *precede* your social media marketing. When you post on social media, you always want to drive traffic to YOUR website, as opposed to someone else's, and having a fresh blog post each week makes it super-easy to do that.

If you're wondering why this is important, think of it this way: When you share someone else's article on social media, it might be helpful, but you're just delivering someone else's content to your followers. In other words, you're a bit like the postal employee delivering someone else's letter.

When you share YOUR content that lives on YOUR website, that traffic comes to YOU and all of the wonderful products and services you offer can be easily found by the reader.

A blog is like a cup of coffee. Anybody can make one, but it takes an understanding of the process — and the right ingredients — to brew something great.

So before we dive into applying SEO, UX and CV into your blog, we're going to consider:
- My efficiency-boosting, stress-reducing blogging processes
- The "premium ingredients" you need to brew a better blog

Once these topics are covered, we'll address how to implement SEO, UX and CV into your blog. What you'll learn is that although some of the applications are quite similar, others are radically different.

Let's start our discussion about blogging with a definition so we're all on the same page ...

WHAT IS A BLOG?
From a global view, a blog is a place where you publish articles online — specifically, on your website.

Whether you're a business connecting with customers and building brand awareness, or an individual talking with your audience, a blog is an effective way to communicate and build *relationships*. A blog can go a long way in making you a trusted, relevant resource. It has the ability to improve engagement and overall reach — plus it's a perfect medium to express oneself, be heard and help others.

A blog can also position you or your organization as an authority, or thought leader, in your industry — adding credibility to your website and team. It's also been known to help people write a full-length book (like the one you're reading)!

And as we'll see, a blog can increase traffic to your website, raise your website authority and improve your ranking in search results.

BREWING A BETTER BLOG
(AKA, MY EFFICIENCY-BOOSTING, STRESS-REDUCING BLOGGING PROCESS)
This all sounds great, but you might be wondering how this is effectively accomplished. So as promised, let's take an in-depth look at Cuppa SEO's blogging process and examine each ingredient you'll need to create an awesome blog.

On the following pages, we'll be covering:

1. What is the purpose of a blog?
2. How to write a blog post in six steps:

1. What is the Purpose of a Blog?

A blog is a fantastic way for a business, individual or group to communicate with readers quickly and easily. It also offers an opportunity for readers to provide instant feedback in a virtual venue, creating a two-way conversation.

Blogs were originally called "web logs," and they've redefined how we communicate online. Blogs have also altered the very fabric of the marketing model, moving us away from a selling philosophy to an era of building relationships.

In a nutshell, building relationships is the purpose of a blog.

How blogs build relationships — the content marketing model

Blogs have altered the very fabric of the marketing model, moving us away from a selling philosophy (thank goodness) and into an era of content marketing, which is a fancy term for building relationships.

As you build relationships, your readers will continue to come back to your blog — and they'll tell their friends or associates about you. Once you've become their trusted source for what you do, you've gained a customer and a brand advocate.

As mentioned earlier, a blog can go a long way toward making you a trusted, relevant resource. And although an occasional "soft" call-to-action on your blog is totally fine, an outright sales pitch is a sure-fire way to ruin your chances of developing a healthy, long-term relationship with your readers.

So instead of the old-fashioned sales pitch many of us were subjected to growing up, use your blog to share rich, relevant, benefit-driven and insightful content — while asking for NOTHING in return. This is one of the best ways to develop relationships online (and in the analog world, too).

2. How to Write a Blog Post (in Six Steps)

I'm often asked how to write a blog post in the most effective way. And although content will vary depending on your industry, customer base and company personality — not to mention your writing style — there are certain criteria you'll want to meet to make sure each of your posts is awesome.

A. The Art of Writing Awesome Blog Titles

In mere seconds, your blog title needs to express what your post is about. It needs to be clear, accurate, as engaging as possible — and honest. In other words, no promising the winning lottery numbers unless you actually know them. Like a good blog post, a good blog title needs to include certain elements ...

Pay Attention to the 3C's

As a writer, I appreciate metaphor and a clever turn of a phrase. But a blog title, also referred to as a headline, needs to make instant sense to your readers. If it's ambiguous or requires too much deduction to figure out, the reader will move on.

A good title can entice a reader to spend a couple of minutes reading your blog. And a good way to benchmark your titles is to ensure they contain what I like to call the 3C's — they need to be clear, compelling and concise.

There's a fourth C, but this one's optional: creative. The reason it's optional? If you're not comfortable "being creative," don't worry about it. Stressing over being creative can be an obstacle that stops you from blogging, so just avoid the pressure! If your blog post contains the 3C's listed above, you'll be just fine.

Crafting the best title possible is important because your headline is a critical element in helping your blog get read. When someone searches for a particular topic, and you are among the list of search engine results, your headline is a deciding factor in whether or not someone clicks through to continue reading. Your headline is also what helps you get found by the search engines in the first place — especially if it's optimized ...

Include a Relevant Keyword Phrase in Blog Titles
Make sure your blog titles contain at least one relevant keyword phrase (when possible).

In the title just above, my keyword phrase is "blog titles," which is searched for 1,000 times per month across the United States. It also has low competition, which means there aren't that many other websites or blogs using this particular phrase.

As we discussed earlier, developing an accurate keyword report helps you determine which keyword phrases are good to use with your blog and your website. Your headline is one of the first places a search engine like Google will look to see what your content is about, making a relevant keyword phrase a must-have.

Make Sure Your Blog Titles are Interesting
This is often the piece of the puzzle that is most perplexing to bloggers. As I mentioned earlier, you as a blog writer can feel pressure to be witty or metaphorical. If you have that talent as a writer, and your brand's voice is in line with this type of communication — go for it. If not, there's a very simple contingency you'll want to meet to ensure that your blog title is interesting: **reveal the value you are presenting in the post.** Whether it's solving a specific problem, opening up a hot topic for discussion, or simply reviewing a movie you saw over the weekend, the title needs to clearly express the value offered within the post.

Even if you rank #1 on Google's natural search results for a particular keyword phrase, your title still needs to engage your readers, or they will click on something else that catches their attention.

B. Make Your Content Rich
OK, so I'm not actually suggesting that you open a bank account for your content. Rich content refers to the quality of the content (copy) you write

in your blog. Writing copy that offers solutions, expert insight and relevant information is rich. In addition, writing about what we're passionate about also tends to result in rich content.

The flip side of this is thin content, which doesn't say anything of importance. Both rich and thin content are recognized by the search engines. Rich content is rewarded, while thin content will move you closer to online obscurity.

When I stepped into the role of content marketing manager for an organization called BizFilings, a division of Wolters Kluwer, BizFilings was blogging TWICE a day, five days a week (way too much!). Blog content was being generated by a third-party content creator who jammed a lot of keywords into content that was pretty much useless. This is thin content at its worst — or should I say thin content at its best?! ; ^)

Anyway, the BizFilings blog was getting fewer than 10 hits a day, which is extremely low for an organization that was pushing out so much content.

The problem: Google knew this content was junk, and it was treated as such. One of my first initiatives was to axe the third-party content creation and pare down the blog post frequency from ten times to three times a week.

And these three posts had to be *rich*. It took about six months of cleanup before Google started perceiving the blog as legitimate again.

When it finally was out of what I call "the black hole of Google Panda," the blog started getting dozens of hits per day — and soon began clocking in at over 100 hits per day! Although not astronomic, going from fewer than 10 hits a day to over 100 is a 1,000% improvement!

C. Be the Expert
Being the expert in your niche makes it easier to write about what's trending in your industry. It will also help you offer relevant solutions to your customers' pain points. Your industry experience can make you an expert in your niche, but constant learning is also a key component. Whether it's from articles, blogs, a mastermind group, or some other medium, fresh input is critical to remaining a thought leader in your industry.

What Do I Write About?

In working with clients and facilitating dozens of workshops on blogging, a common question often arises: What do I write about?

And no matter what type of business you run, the answer is always the same:

Write about what you know.

In other words, write about your area of expertise. What do you know more about and get more excited about than almost anyone else on the planet?

More often than not, I've found that people who are experts in their industry often feel that they have nothing to write about. They don't feel like an expert, or they believe nobody would want to read what they have to say.

Although there can be multiple reasons for these concerns, there's one thing I'd like to share: To you, what you do every day feels commonplace; it has become natural to you, so it's easy to believe that everyone has the same information and depth of understanding that you do.

This is simply not true. Trust me. You've probably worked for years to become really good at what you do, and the depth or breadth of knowledge you have is BRAND NEW to the rest of us who don't do what you do. Sharing this knowledge can be super helpful — and has great value — to your clients. And that's what a blog is all about — sharing relevant, useful information with people who want and need it.

Think about it: You know what your customers' biggest problems and pain points are. You know *exactly* how your products and/or services can solve their problems. The only difference is that instead of discussing these pain points and solutions face-to-face with a client, you need to put that knowledge into words and write about it on your blog.

So if you're thinking "Why would anybody want to read what I have to say?" The answer is the same reason your clients come to you in the first place: You have something of value to offer.

Remember, things that are commonplace to you, are NOT commonplace to your clients! And I don't know anybody who finds a solution to one of their problems boring or irrelevant, do you?

In my industry, clients want to know more about SEO, user experience (UX), web design, conversion (CV), blogging and social media. Each of these main topics has many, many subtopics that I can focus on in a blog post, giving me hundreds of things to write about.

Being the expert is possibly the most important of all the blogging tips I share, because a blog cannot exist without content. And it will never engage with readers unless that content is relevant and useful. You — with your expertise — can generate that content for your readers.

D. Use an Engaging Image
No blog post is complete without imagery. Make sure yours is interesting, relevant and large enough to make an impact. Although every blog is different, an image size of somewhere around 350-400px wide usually does the trick.

You don't have to spend a lot of money on your images, but you do have to spend some time to find or create good imagery. Although it's always preferred to use original imagery or art, there are companies like iStockPhoto that provide an immense number of options. Just make sure what you choose doesn't look like a stock photo!

If you're not a designer but want to make your own images, check out the App Store (iOS/Mac) or Google Play (Android/Chrome on PC or Mac), and search for "photo editing," "graphics" or "add text to photos" for a bunch of inexpensive or free options to get you started. My favorite iOS app is called Over, and it's pretty powerful.

E. Keep it Short, or Not!
When it comes to preferred blog post length, there is no single right answer. My general advice is to say what you've got to say in as few words as possible without compromising your message or brand voice. Generally, somewhere around 500 words can be a sweet spot for length. It's not too short or too long, but 500 words is enough to get at least one solid point

across. That being said, if your topic or writing style calls for longer or shorter posts, be sure to honor that and adjust the blog length accordingly.

Why Your Blog Might be Shorter
Let's face it — we live in a digital age where tweets and texts have altered how we communicate. Our busy schedules often don't allow for time to read long blog posts. A blogger's challenge is to be succinct and informational, while at the same time being able to tell an engaging story or at least add some personality to each post. And to blog regularly.

Knowing your brand, your writing style AND YOUR READER will dictate whether or not short blog posts are a good solution. Like my grammar school English teacher, Ms. Krebs, used to say, "Anything is better than a zero." In other words, if you have time for only a 150-word post, write it and publish it. It will do more good to maintain a regular blog schedule of posts of varied lengths than publishing nothing or publishing sporadically.

And if you're really pressed for time, I've created something even shorter than 150 words that will require only 20–30 minutes of your time to complete and publish. It's called a bleet®.

What is a bleet?

A bleet is the marriage of a blog post and a tweet — resulting in an opportunity to express yourself in 420 characters or less, including spaces (that's triple the original character count of a tweet).

The idea is to offer more substance than a tweet, while keeping your content extremely short. Because you can write a bleet quickly, it's easier to express yourself more often. Characters in your title count, too.

Why Your Blog Might be Longer
Of course there are exceptions, and some readers expect long-form content from certain industries. There are also instances where long-form posts, what I like to call a "deep dive," can be a differentiator in helping you rise above your competition.

For instance, let's say your competitors are typically writing 500-word posts about a subject, which allows them to only skim the surface of a topic. If you write a deep dive post — say 1,200 to 2,000 words — that offers in-depth information on the topic, you're positioning yourself as more knowledgeable on the topic. But again, it depends on your industry and what your readers' expectations are.

Do remember that there's definitely still a place for long-form blogs.

No matter what length your blog posts end up being, as long as you're consistently blogging at least once a week, you'll see your blog traffic increase — and along with it your reputation as an expert.

F. Create a Blog Campaign (Pick Your Topics)
One of the top comments I receive during every Blogging 101 webinar or workshop is that people find the thought of blogging stressful. This is understandable, especially if you've never blogged before, because the entire process is one big question mark.

But fear not! I'm going to share a proven process that shows you how to create a monthly blog campaign that makes blogging *more* fun and *less* stressful!

Schedule Time
Just like you'd schedule an appointment with a client, your dentist or your doctor, schedule time for yourself to create a monthly blog campaign. Take out (now!) your analog or digital calendar, and schedule one hour exclusively for blog-campaign creation. Treat this appointment with the respect you would any other.

Schedule time in April to work on your May blog posts. In May, schedule time for your June blog posts (and so on). You always want to create your campaigns a month in advance. This approach relieves the stress when you actually begin to write your blog, because you have given your brain time with the subject matter — either consciously or unconsciously — making it easier to create the blog post.

Choose Your Blog Topics and Titles
You don't need to plan every detail; just try to think of 4–5 blog topics for

the next month, and write a tentative title for each. I know what you're thinking: "What should my blog topics be about?" The answer is easier than you may think. Topics should address the pain points and struggles your customers are experiencing (as we discussed earlier). In other words, your blog topics can be about the questions and problems your clients talk with you about ... those that you help them solve.

Remember: It's easy to fall into the trap of thinking you have nothing of value to say. Solving problems in your area of expertise is what you do every day — it's commonplace to you. But it's not commonplace to your customers!

Write a 2–3 Sentence Overview
Think of this as the CliffsNotes version for each of your blog posts. What exactly is it about? Can you write three sentences — one for the beginning, the middle and the end of your post? This brief overview does NOT need to be polished; it just needs to be clear and relevant.

If you think you're going to need to research a particular topic, it's a good idea to pull together 2-3 pieces of online material (other blog posts, articles or websites) that you can review before writing your post. Copy/paste the URL with your notes so that if you're quoting or heavily referring to one of these sources, you can easily cite the source in your blog post.

Save, Smile, and Treat Yourself to a Coffee!
When you've completed the above steps, you're nearly done with your planning session. Make sure you clearly name and save the document ... something like, "Blog Campaign for May 2019." Create a "Blogging" folder for saving your drafts. There's nothing worse than doing all this prep, and then not being able to find your work. Next, brew up a fresh cup of coffee and enjoy!

When the next month rolls around, you'll know exactly what you will be blogging about each week ... no more staring at a blank page under pressure, wondering what to do. You'll be amazed at how much easier — and fun — blogging can be!

3. What are Tags and Categories?
Tags and categories have been known to confound new bloggers. The good news is that they appear a lot more confusing than they actually are.

Let's take a look at each and how to use them in your blog posts.

Because tags and categories aren't part of the actual body of your blog post, they can easily be overlooked. But if you want to write a successful blog, you'll want to make sure you include them correctly in every post.

Blog Tags
While working on your blog in WordPress, you'll notice a region on the right-hand side of the page that looks similar to the image below. This is where your tags go for the post you're currently creating.

But What are Tags, and How do They Work?
Tags are keywords or keyword phrases that are placed in the tags region in the WordPress editor of your blog. Here's what the input box looks like in WordPress:

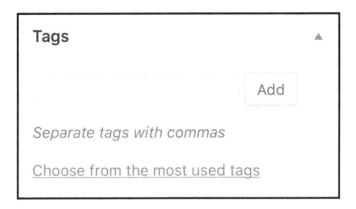

The format of this box may vary, depending on your WordPress theme, but the information should be the same.

Tags are for search engines. They let Google, Bing and other search engines know what keywords you'd like them to look for in your post. In essence, you're reminding the search engines to pay attention to a handful of keywords because they're important.

Make sure you list no more than 5 keyword phrases in your tags area. And make sure that these phrases all appear, at least a few times, in the blog post itself — or you won't really get any credit for them as keywords.

Blog Categories

Categories are for the human eye. That's it. Google doesn't pay attention to them in any valuable way, but they're critical to your readers. When you add a phrase to the categories section on your blog (again while you're on the editor side, working on a blog post), you're actually bucketing blog posts into a particular — you guessed it — category. Here's an image of what the categories box looks like in WordPress:

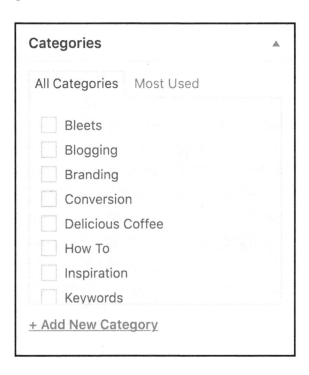

What you enter here is typically visible to your visitors on the right-side navigation of your blog. It may be a vertical list of topics, or it may be a "cloud-like" listing.

Again, search engines don't care about your categories, but people might. If they're well-constructed, categories can help readers find additional blog posts you've written that might be of interest to them. For example, someone reading a post of mine about SEO might want to read more posts about SEO. Because I have an SEO category, I've made it easy for them to peruse all of my posts that have to do with the subject of search engine optimization, or any of the other major categories I write about ...

Categories

- Bleets
- Blogging
- Branding
- Conversion
- Delicious Coffee
- How To
- Inspiration
- Keywords
- Marketing
- Networking
- SEO
- Social Media
- User Experience (UX)
- Videos
- Web Design

Categories help visitors find what they're looking for — and can lead to more of your blog posts being read. Try to limit your total of Categories to 15 or fewer. To accomplish this, make sure each category — or bucket — is broad enough to contain a variety of topics that you write about, while still being specific enough to understand at a glance.

On a final note, there might be times when you use the same keyword phrase for a tag and a category. That's totally OK! They can be the same when it's appropriate. Just make sure you populate both the tags and categories sections on your blog.

Remember, *tags* are for *search engines*, and *categories* are for *readers*.

4. Blog Post Frequency

Now we're going to cover optimal blog post frequency, another piece of the SEO pie that needs to be understood so it can be used effectively to improve your website authority and reach more readers.

So you've decided to start blogging, and you're wondering how often you need to blog. Once a month? Five times a week? What is the "magic number" that's going to help increase your reach AND improve your website's authority?

You'll be glad to know that blogging just once a week can help you accomplish both of these goals. But it's got to be consistent, week after week.

That being said, while one blog post per week is considerably better than none, two is twice as good, and the sweet spot for most businesses is actually three times per week.

Why? Because it provides your blog (and your website) with the perfect amount of fresh content each week. More than three posts per week can often be perceived as too much by the search engines — and by your readers.

I can guess what you're thinking: "Joey, how the heck are we going to produce three blog post per week?" It's why I suggest that you start off by shooting for one post per week. The goal: Make things as manageable as possible so you actually DO it. And if you follow my previous advice and create a blog campaign, you'll improve your odds for success considerably.

And as you publish one blog post per week — week after week — Google will notice. In fact, every time Google "crawls" your website, it will see your new blog post and say, "fresh content, woo-hoo!" The result? Your authority with Google and other search engines will rise, as will your search ranking.

5. The Freshness Factor
Although we talked about it early in the book as part of the SEO equation, let's talk a little more about the importance of fresh content on your website.

When you start writing a blog, it becomes the source for your site's fresh content, which is very appealing to Google. In addition to pleasing Google, fresh content is also very appealing to the human eye — which is why a blog is so effective in building relationships.

Part of Google's algorithm is called Penguin, and it looks at your website to determine if there's fresh content there. As discussed earlier, if you're blogging regularly, Google takes notice and gives you a little extra authority. If not, your authority can go in the other direction.

The Right Way to Freshen Your Website Content
You might be wondering why I keep stressing that fresh content should be associated with your blog. It's because *where* you add fresh content to your site is just as important as how rich, relevant and optimized it is.

Many novice SEO practitioners will tell you that the best way to inject new content into your site is to "freshen up" your homepage and subpages with new copy and keyword phrases — often on a monthly basis.

Taking this approach on a well-optimized website isn't only ineffective; it's downright harmful, because ...

SEO is Like a Phone Number
Why is constantly freshening up your actual web pages a bad idea? Let me ask you this:

Would you change your phone number each month?

Of course not. Customers and colleagues are depending on your being on the other end of a specific set of ten digits when they make a call to get in touch. It's the same with Google, which is counting on more than your URL for a particular page's location — but also the optimized title tag, headline, imagery, content and text links that live on each web page.

Just like when you dial a phone number, you expect a specific person or business to be on the other end, Google is expecting to find you based on the information you've implemented with your SEO. And when you change the information — changing a phone number, for example — you're no longer where Google expects you to be. When this happens, it's like hitting the metaphorical reset button on your website, losing valuable website authority in the process. In other words, you could lose some or all of your website authority by changing your homepage and subpage SEO in an effort to freshen up your content.

This is why fresh content needs to go on your blog!

Case Study: Cuppa SEO's Blog

You might be wondering just how much weight a consistent blog post — written week-in-and-week-out — carries. Although I had cultivated many blogs to robust health, I had never tested the effects of removing a consistent stream of fresh content from a healthy blog. So I decided to conduct a test on the Cuppa SEO blog. Here's what happened ...

- Before the experiment, Cuppa SEO ranked 1st & 2nd on page one of Google's search results for my top keyword phrases.
- I stopped blogging completely for 15 weeks — don't try this at home!
- After about 90 days (12 weeks), my position started to slip, and after 15 weeks my ranking slipped to the bottom of page one, or to page two, for my keyword phrases.
- When I started blogging again, I began to improve my ranking after I consistently published a few new blog posts.
- After nine weeks of weekly blogging again, I started ranking on page one again for my top keyword phrases. It took additional time for me to regain my position on the top of the page, but eventually I was #1 or #2 again!

As you can see, the simple act of blogging can have a dramatic influence on where your website ranks in a Google search. The higher you rank, the more likely the chance that customers will find you — which of course means more business.

Social Media Side Note: When I wasn't blogging, I didn't have new content to share on social media, which meant that I wasn't engaging as much with my followers — and I wasn't getting SEO value from my social media channels. Like anything else in life, doing or not doing just one thing can have an effect on many other things. Now you have yet one more reason to blog! OK, I'll step down off my soapbox ...

6. Original Content vs. Duplicate Content

In some ways, the difference between these two types of content is obvious. But there can be ambiguity connected to duplicate content, so let's take a closer look.

Original Content

This one's pretty straightforward. Original content is exactly what you'd think: made from scratch, unique, one of a kind. It's content that you've written yourself, even if that means you've researched other material (which you can cite in your blog post) for the information. Google likes this type of content, and so do readers.

Duplicate Content

Have you ever heard of a "carbon copy"? In the days before copy machines or printers, we wrote or typed on a plain sheet of paper that had a piece of carbon paper between it and a second sheet of paper, creating a duplicate. This is a good way to think of duplicate content, which is something you'll want to avoid using on your blog.

Many bloggers I know like to highlight other bloggers. They'll find a fantastic article, decide to share it, and post it verbatim on their own blog with a link to the original blogger's site. Although ethically this is completely fine, search engines will probably interpret this "carbon-copy repost" as duplicate content.

Now, you might be wondering, "What does that mean, oh Caffeinated One?" Well, let me tell you …

If Google sees that you've posted someone else's content on your site, and you include a backlink to the original content, it's unlikely that you'll receive any kind of penalty — but you also won't receive any credit for fresh content, which means the post won't do much for your website authority.

There's a misconception that Google will ding you for reposting someone else's work. In truth, unless Google deems your site as intentionally trying to manipulate search engine results, it won't get mad at you. It simply won't give you credit for fresh content. Google will try its best to discern which blog post is the original … and since each blog post has a date stamp, it will be pretty obvious that yours is a duplicate.

So, what do you do if you want to highlight someone else's blog post — and get credit for fresh content?

Summarize what the highlighted blog post is about in one or two paragraphs. Then add your authentic opinion to the mix. Finally, place a backlink in your blog post that leads readers to the full post you're highlighting.

Now you've effectively highlighted the information AND shown your expertise by chiming in with your insights. You've also created a backlink that can help boost the authority of the blog/website you're linking to — and all the while you've avoided creating duplicate content.

Holistic Side Note: Whenever you're highlighting somebody else's work or using someone's work as the basis of your research, you'll want to cite them in your blog post. It's not only a common courtesy; it's the ethically sound choice.

That being said, my opinion on backlinks has changed over the years. While I always used to include a backlink to the original content in my blog post, I do so much less these days. The reason is simple: If I include a backlink to the original content and someone clicks on it, THEY'VE LEFT MY BLOG, AND THEY MIGHT NOT COME BACK.

There's a simple, yet critical rule every good web designer follows: Once you get someone to your blog or website, you want to keep them there. Offering a shiny object like a link to someone else's content, or a link to your social media pages (discussed in more detail later in this book) is a big no-no.

Instead, as we've discussed, we want to create a great user experience, coupled with clear and compelling conversion strategies that keep visitors on the path to developing a relationship with us.

7. Setting Up Your Blog as a Subpage (GOOD) vs. a Subdomain (BAD)

In order for your blog to count as fresh content on your website, it has to be a *subpage* of your site, not a *subdomain*. This can be confusing, so let's clear things up with a couple of quick definitions, along with a visual example.

When your blog is a subpage of your main URL, it's actually part of the site and supports your overall website authority.

When your blog is a subdomain, it's actually a completely different website that *competes* with your main website.

Here's an example of what a URL would look like for a subpage and a subdomain. Once you know what to look for, it's easy to spot the difference.

Subpage vs. Subdomain

Subpage: www.YourWebsiteURL.com/blog/

Subdomain: www.blog.YourWebsiteURL.com

---

8. Scheduling Blog Posts

What happens if you're the type of blogger who likes to write more than one blog post at a time ... or you find yourself getting a few weeks ahead on your blog ... or you're planning to go on vacation, and you don't want to interrupt your blog publishing schedule?

You learn to schedule your blog posts! Scheduling allows you to completely prepare a post so it's ready to go — but it won't publish until the time you designate. Let's take a quick look at how to do this ...

Once you're logged into WordPress and you've started working on a new blog post, you'll find the scheduling option under the Publishing tab on the right side of the page. If the tab isn't already expanded, click on the arrow in the upper right corner. You should then see the following:

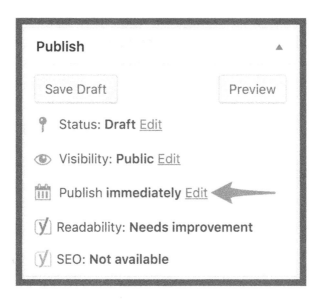

By default, your blog post is set to publish immediately. But if you click on the edit button, you have full control of when the post will actually go live:

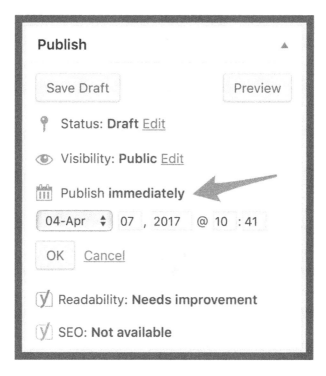

Once you're done, be sure to click the "OK" button, and then click on the "Schedule" button to complete the process. When the day and time you scheduled arrives, your post will publish.

Once it's published, be sure to share your latest content on social media!

Holistic Side Note — Blog Subscriptions: Many moons ago, there was a blog subscription service called Feedburner that worked really well for allowing visitors to sign up (subscribe) for email updates whenever the subscriber published a new blog post. Although Feedburner still exists, it was purchased by Google and lost much of its functionality.

But there are lots of paid and free options that make it possible for visitors to sign up for email notifications when you publish a post. If you're looking for something super-simple to capture subscriber info and automatically email them your latest content, Jetpack (a free, rather robust WordPress plugin), has a free subscriptions app built right in.

Once implemented, a widget is created that sits on the right-hand side of your blog ...

All your visitors have to do is enter their email address, and they're signed up. There is, however, a downside to the Jetpack plugin: There doesn't seem to be an easy way to integrate it with an email application like MailChimp.

In addition to the Jetpack widget, I also like to create a nice button that sits at the bottom of each blog post. If somebody finishes an informative, satisfying blog post, he or she can easily subscribe to receive more! Here's what Cuppa SEO's subscribe button looks like ...

Once clicked, it prompts the visitor to "subscribe to this blog and receive notifications of new posts by email."

9. The Role of Social Media in Blogging (a Prelude to Part 4)

I'm not a big fan of social media buttons that drive people to your actual social media platforms. As we discussed earlier, social media is a tool that should drive visitors TO your website, not AWAY from it! I *am* a big fan of blog sharing, which is different. With blog sharing, a visitor remains on your website while sharing a blog post on a social media channel by using a pop-up window. This functionality can easily be integrated into a WordPress site with one of many plugins, and will look something like this ...

Now that you have a solid understanding of how blogging works, it's time to address how to implement SEO, UX and CV into your blog. And that's exactly what the next three chapters cover ...

9. SEO and Your Blog

Implementation of SEO into your blog mirrors what we covered in Chapter 1: *What is SEO?*, and Chapter 5: *Search Engine Optimization,* which covered how to apply SEO to your website.

If you've read these chapters, you are in excellent shape to start applying SEO to your blog!

Let's begin by taking a look at an example to refresh your memory. Just as we did in the SEO section, let's review the six major areas of a blog post where you'll want to implement your SEO efforts. For more detailed analysis of each of these points, please refer to Chapter 5 ...

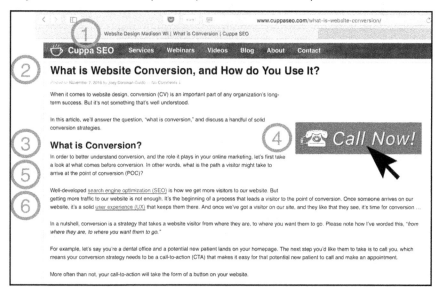

1. Title Tags

These are the words (content) in the gray bar at the very top of a web page. Best practices dictate that these should be no longer than 70 characters long, including spaces and "sticks." For blog posts, the title tag is usually the blog post title, or a variant of the title, with your company name at the end, as depicted in the example on the previous page.

2 & 3. Headlines

Implementing relevant keywords into each headline can help clarify what your blog is about. It can also help increase the SEO value of your post.

This action includes ALL types of headlines, but the three most widely used are:

- #2 in our example is an H1 Headline — this is the primary headline in a blog post. You should use only ONE H1 headline per blog post.
- #3 in the example is an H3 Headline — smaller, "third-tier" headlines that can appear more than once in a blog post.
- A third fairly popular headline type is the H2 Headline — which, when used, is the secondary headline that can appear in a blog post, very often just below the H1.

4. Image & Alternate Image Text (Also Referred to as Alt Text)

Optimizing your image names and alternate image text is just as important in blog posts as on your homepage and subpages.

When I'm writing a blog post, I often like to include additional images throughout the post to support/clarify the learnings I'm sharing in the content. Not only does it make things easier to comprehend and more engaging for readers; it's also a great opportunity to add additional optimization to the blog post.

5. Content

In addition to writing great content, you'll also need to use primary, secondary and semantic keywords (discussed in Chapter 5) in each blog post. Incorporate them in an organic way where they make sense through-out the post. And just as with your homepage and subpages — no stuffing!

6. Descriptive Links

Descriptive links, also referred to as text links, are part of your content and need to be optimized whenever possible.

Text links are typically links that ask visitors to take action — to learn more, schedule an appointment, make a purchase, and so on. Simply stating something like "learn more," misses an opportunity to give Google — and the reader — good, clear information. A well-crafted text link should include at least one keyword phrase whenever possible.

Bonus Section: Meta Descriptions

Although they don't have SEO value, meta descriptions have value to the human eye. Each meta description should read like a complete sentence (or two short sentences) and be no longer than 156 characters, including spaces and punctuation. If you go past 156 characters, the viewer will see an ellipsis that essentially cuts off the rest of your message, and Google doesn't like that.

10. User Experience and Your Blog

When it comes to UX on your blog, most of the principles we discussed in Part 2 for desktop and mobile subpages hold true. The only real difference relates to how we handle a call-to-action.

That said, here's a quick review of what a good user experience looks like on a blog ...

Content and Imagery

First, let's take a look at the actual content and imagery on the left side. After that, we'll briefly review the boxes (typically referred to as "widgets") on the right.

1. *Headline:* This is your PRIMARY headline for the page, which is referred to on the editor side of the blog as an H1. It should sit at the top of the page. To accomplish this, simply implement your H1 into this region ...

2. *Page Content (copy):* You'll want your page content to be large enough to read on both desktop and mobile. Be sure to use an easy-to-read font like Helvetica, and keep your paragraphs short so they're easy to digest. Another tip: Make your font color black. WordPress often sets the default color of text to gray, which is harder to read because it offers less contrast. This might appear to be a small thing, but why make your text harder to read? That's bad for UX!

3. *H3 Headlines:* In contrast to H1s, you can use as many H3s as you like in a blog post. H3s serve as subheads and are an excellent way to segment your content, making it easier for readers to home in on exactly what they want to read. In the example here, the H3s show readers — at a glance — what each section of the blog post is about ("FTP vs. FTPS," and "HTTP vs. HTTPS") so they don't have to scan or read the whole article if they're interested in only one section.

4. *Imagery:* In addition to the SEO value it can provide (as long as you optimize it), blog post imagery also serves other purposes. It adds visual interest to the blog post, and it helps break up the page so it's not all words. In addition to the "hero image" you see at the top of our current example, I'll often use additional images throughout the post to visually support what I'm writing about. Just make sure every image you use has relevance to the blog post and isn't there just for the sake of adding imagery. And, as in our example, justify your hero image at the top of the post to the right. When you do so, the copy on the page wraps more neatly (than if you were to place the image on the left) for a better user experience.

Right-side Widgets

Let's move on to what we see on the right side of the Cuppa SEO blog. These boxes of information are called widgets, and there's a lot of customization that you can employ with them. You can change their order of appearance, or you can selectively remove some. These options help you set up your blog in a way that makes sense to your readers. Are they more interested in reviewing your categories, recent posts, archives, or something else? That said, it's always a good idea to lead off your widgets with ...

1. *Your Search Box:* A search box makes it easy for a visitor to find information on a specific blog topic. Placing it in the upper-right corner of your blog makes it easy to find (that's where people expect it to be), hence providing a good UX.

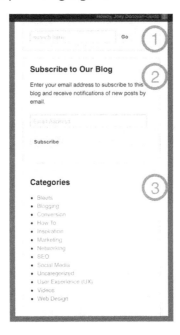

2. *Subscribe:* When someone likes your blog, there's a chance that person might want to subscribe to it. Make it easy with a subscribe widget right under your search box! And make it as easy as possible to fill out by requiring only an email address, or possibly a name as well. To accomplish this, use a subscribe WordPress plugin that doesn't ask users to join or have an account in order to receive your latest blog posts. I use the free, built-in subscription service

that lives in the Jetpack plugin. There are many others of various robustness to choose from.

3. *Categories:* Here's where those categories we spoke about earlier come into play. Make sure they're crystal clear and well defined, as they're a visitor's portal to more content you've written on a particular subject. Remember to keep your category count as low as possible. In other words, you don't want a couple of dozen categories in your list, as that's too many to easily sift through. Create big "umbrella" categories — SEO, for example — where many similar categories such as keywords, Google My Business and other SEO-centric topics can live.

4. *Recent Posts:* Next up on the Cuppa SEO blog is Recent Posts, which is exactly what it sounds like: a listing of only the titles of the last few published posts.

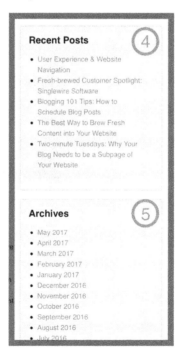

5. *Archives* is next, and it's where all of our older posts are stored and bucketed together month by month. You'd be surprised at how quickly you wind up with a long list of blog posts after consistently blogging once a week!

There are a lot more widgets you can add to your right-hand side bar, and depending on your niche, you might want to consider some of them in addition to, or instead of, what I've detailed here. Just remember to always consider the user experience of every aspect of your blog, and take steps to make it as positive as possible. If you're not sure what's best, ask a handful of trusted clients for their opinion.

Full Blog Posts vs. Excerpts

When it comes to how you present your blog to the world, you have two options — show full blog posts, or show excerpts. I have always preferred to show full blog posts, as it presents a simpler user experience: There's only one post to look at when you arrive on the blog.

The potential problem with this method is *there's only one post to look at when you arrive on the blog.* If site visitors are not interested in that particular topic, they have to scroll to see additional posts, which can complicate the user experience. So full blog posts can, at times, provide a better UX, while at other times. the full blog post can provide a less-desirable UX.

That said, I've done a small UX test, and most of the people I worked with preferred to arrive on a blog that presents excerpts, "so a handful of posts can be scanned quickly." Because of the results the test provided, I've changed my blog to show excerpts, which look like this ...

Web Design Tips: Avoid Carousels (Slideshows)

Posted on February 4, 2017 by Joey Donovan-Guido · 1 Comment ↓

Website carousels, also referred to as slideshows or rotating offers, are something we find on a lot of websites. But they're a bad user experience and they're bad for conversion. As an organization, it's always tempting to give MORE information ...

Read more ›

Tagged with: web design, Web Design Madison WI, Website Carousels
Posted in Conversion, User Experience (UX), Web Design

THE MOBILE VERSION OF YOUR BLOG

Again, just as with your website subpages, the mobile version of your blog needs to be different from the desktop version for an optimal user experience. Here's a look at the same blog post on mobile that we examined earlier.

Here's what you see first:

Scrolling down, you see:

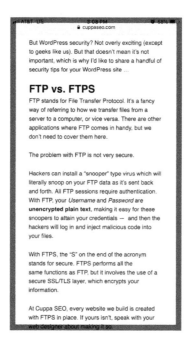

On mobile (at least on a smartphone), because there's no room for a sidebar on the right, all of the widgets we discussed earlier should cascade to the bottom of the post. They'll remain in the same order as they appear on desktop view, but the smaller screen size dictates that they live in a different place. Sometimes you'll visit a blog on your phone that shows these widgets at the top, or if the blog isn't mobile friendly, it might show ALL of the info just as you see it on a desktop screen. In both cases, this is bad for UX!

11. Conversion and Your Blog

Conversion strategy on your blog is very different from the strategy employed on your homepage and subpages. Why? Because on your actual website pages, in addition to building relationships and connecting with visitors, we're trying to get those visitors to take the next step. Your homepage and some (or many) of your subpages should be designed to convert visitors to take an action: contact you, download an ebook, schedule an appointment, buy a service or product, etc.

I don't like to look at these as selling tactics, because I believe nobody likes to be "sold." Instead, these are relationship-building strategies that sometimes lead to people converting to the next step. That said, it's still a pretty direct process ... if you need what I do, please call me so we can talk ... If you need a root canal, schedule an appointment ...

With your blog, the goal is different. Remember what we talked about earlier?

The purpose of a blog is building relationships.

It's where you build trust, credibility, and where you build your reputation as a thought leader and expert in your field. Your blog is the place where you provide relevant information, solutions and insights — while asking for *nothing* in return.

This is why conversion has a different flavor on your blog as opposed to conversion on your homepage or subpages.

In a way, the relationship-building model we're talking about here *IS* the conversion strategy for your blog — but it's a slow burn. Think about it. If you're providing great information week after week on your blog, when one of your readers needs what you do — whom do you think they're going to call? OK, other than the Ghostbusters? That's right — YOU, because they already know you're an expert they can trust.

Now, I'm not saying you can never have a call-to-action in a blog post, but it shouldn't be a big contrast-colored button at the top of the page. Instead, a call-to-action — if you use one at all in a post — typically sits at the bottom of the blog in the form of a text link.

In the following blog post, *Web Design & the Art of Conversion*, I take the reader through "traditional" conversion strategy, and how — through design — we can radically alter that strategy and still get excellent results. The entire article is devoted to discussing this point.

But because it's a post about web design, which is a large part of our business, I included a "soft" call-to-action as my conversion strategy at the end of the post ...

> We hope these concepts help you think differently about your conversion strategies and the design elements of our homepage.
>
> *Need help with conversion strategies?*
> Contact Cuppa SEO to schedule a complimentary consultation, very possibly over a cup of coffee!

As you can see, I kept the call-to-action light and friendly, pressure-free, clear and short.

There are times when having a soft call-to-action somewhere closer to the top of a blog post might be appropriate. If you're overviewing one of your whitepapers in a blog post, for example, you might want to add a text link right after the overview that says something like, "Download the Whitepaper."

In this case, your call-to-action is an *extension* of the information you're sharing. In other words, MORE relevant information on the topic — but still with NO strings attached.

This conversion philosophy holds true on both desktop and mobile.

Now that we've covered all of the components of blogging, let's talk about the role of social media.

PART 4: SOCIAL MEDIA

Now that your blog is up and running (yay!), it's finally time to learn how to apply SEO, UX and conversion into your social media.

Before we move on, it's time to take a breath and acknowledge that we've covered a lot of ground. To begin, we gained a solid understanding of SEO, user experience and conversion. Then we covered — in a specific order — how to apply these disciplines first to your website and then your blog before we began our discussion of applying them to social.

That time is finally here, so let's get social! We'll begin by answering a common question ...

WHY WAIT TO IMPLEMENT A SOCIAL MEDIA PLAN?
The reason social media is last on our online marketing to-do list is actually very simple; you'll want to use social to drive visitors to your website and blog — not to content written by someone else.

In order to do this, you need rich, relevant content on your website — while providing a good user experience and solid conversion. In addition to publishing social media posts that lead to products and services pages (which is sometimes a good idea), it's your blog that will provide a wealth of fresh, relevant content to share on your social media channels.

Using social media this way helps increase traffic to your website and blog. But there are other perks. It also helps position you as an expert and thought leader — and it can help increase the authority of your website as a whole (especially if visitors are liking, sharing or commenting on your blog posts), which means you'll rank higher in natural search results.

As with your website and blog content, your social media content needs to be rich, relevant — and benefit driven. Remember: If you're solving someone's pain point, they're much more likely to click through to read more. If you're telling them about your latest award, there's a high probability they won't care.

Chapters in this part of the book dive into the following topics:

- An overview of social media
- In-depth discussion of three major social media platforms:
  - Google My Business
  - LinkedIn
  - Facebook

For each of these platforms we'll cover:

- How to use SEO to optimize each platform on a page level
- Page-level UX and conversion strategies
- How to implement SEO, UX and conversion strategies directly into every social media post you publish

Our overview begins with the two sides of social media ...

12. An Overview of Social Media

THE TWO SIDES OF SOCIAL MEDIA
Just like a coin, there are two sides (or purposes) to social media:

1. To connect with *people* and develop relationships
2. To connect with *Google* and boost your SEO value

Here's our hi-tech graphic that breaks it down further ...

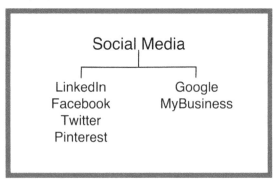

Connecting with People
Platforms such as Facebook, LinkedIn and Twitter are for human-to-human interaction. They're great for building relationships, brand awareness, and for highlighting products or services with actual people.

In each post, you'll want to include some SEO strategies — use of optimal keywords in content and imagery, for example — to help clients and potential clients find you (more on this later). But keep in mind that these channels don't hold the lion's share of SEO value. Let's talk about which one does ...

Connecting with Google

Through research and testing, I've found that Google My Business (GMB) does hold the lion's share of SEO value when it comes to social media. Although things have changed since Google+ was taken out of the equation, we're finding GMB still has a lot more SEO juice than any other social network.

Holistic Side Note: At one point in time, Google+ was part of the Google My Business SEO equation, but it became a lame duck in October 2018 when Google announced its demise.

That said, publishing posts through GMB is key if you want to increase the authority of your website, your blog — and your actual GMB listing (which is the map/business listing you sometimes see in search results).

The good news is that you don't need to write new content for GMB. All you need to do to gain some traction is to publish the same content and imagery you're publishing on your other social media platforms.

WOULD THE GHOSTBUSTERS NEED SOCIAL MEDIA?

© Cuppa SEO

In today's golden age of online marketing, the answer to this question would certainly be yes, although a better question would be HOW should the Ghostbusters use social media, and WHO should be creating the content?

In order to know how to proceed, the Ghostbusters would have to answer the same questions as would any other business:

1. What social media channels are our customers and potential customers using?
2. What are their pain points?
3. What benefits of our product or service do they care about the most?
4. What kind of content will resonate with them? Remember, we want engagement, not a one-way conversation!

And before any social media campaign begins — or any marketing collateral is created, for that matter — another important question must be answered:

What does the voice of our brand sound like?

Voice is more than tone; it's the embodiment of your company's personality.

Imagine for a moment that the Ghostbusters are sitting around the dinner table in the firehouse eating cold Chinese food (or maybe some Cheez-It crackers). They're debating about who should handle their Facebook page. You've got four distinct personalities, all of which will appeal to a particular customer niche ...

RAY: the playful, child-like geek who still gets excited about the intersection of technology and the paranormal.

PETER: the sharp-tongued, quick-witted charmer who essentially has no filter.

WINSTON: the good-hearted guy who appeals to the non-geek crowd; he's the everyman who fell into a job that happened to include wearing an unlicensed nuclear accelerator on his back.

EGON: my personal favorite, Egon will most likely want to discuss his fungus and mold-spore collection while delivering dead-pan humor with a sly smile.

Depending on their audience, any of these personalities could be a winner. My initial feeling is that all four should be working on their social media as a team, testing their efforts and seeing what's gaining the most traction and engagement. If nothing else, there would be variety and richness to their campaigns that none of the four could accomplish themselves.

On the other hand, if 90% of their customer base is interested in mold spores, then maybe the rest of the team should just stick to catching ghosts.

In the end, this section of the book isn't meant to offer one clear answer about your social media. It's meant to make you *think about your own business*, how you're currently handling your social media efforts, and how a shift in the way you communicate just might help you engage with more people.

YOUR SOCIAL MEDIA IS NOT YOU ...

... It may resemble you, and it may sound like you. But in the end, your social media is only a very thin sliver of who you actually are. The real you is far more robust and interesting.

The truth is that social media was never meant to be a replacement for live, in-person handshaking and networking. Instead it's a complementary tactic, a supportive endeavor — at least on a local level.

Don't get me wrong, you can attract a good amount of business from well-conceived social media efforts — especially when you're sharing relevant info or having a dialog on the social media channels where your customers spend their time. But if you're a company that does business locally, you can, at least to some extent, still get a fair share of clients from in-person networking. Of course, you've got to know which groups to network in, which might take some trial and error.

Avoiding the Hungry Wolf Syndrome

Have you ever been to a networking event where you've seen someone suffering from "hungry wolf syndrome?" Have you ever suffered from it yourself?

Classic signs are a tad of wildness in the eyes, a bit of a snarl — even some drooling might be apparent — creating an appearance of desperation to make a sale or land a customer that makes the person resemble a hungry wolf whose only concern is finding his next meal. Avoid this syndrome at all costs because people will see you coming from a mile away!

You're much better off going to a networking event with one simple goal in mind:

Develop relationships.

The great thing about this philosophy is that it holds true online, too, from the creation of a successful website, to your blog and social media campaigns. Some of the relationships you develop will lead to learnings, some to friendships, some to customers — and some to people you'll never want to talk to again. ; ^)

When your intention is to develop relationships, you can be your authentic self, not your "selling self." And if you're developing healthy relationships, when someone you know needs a service or product you provide, there's a very good chance that person will come to you. You might even get a recommendation or two.

So, unless you're Duran Duran, don't be hungry like the wolf.

13. Google My Business (GMB)

Let's start our social media deep dive with Google My Business. I'll begin with this platform because I've found it to be the least understood — and the most confusing to business owners. As mentioned earlier, it's the most important social platform for SEO, and it's critical for local businesses to have a fully optimized listing.

> **Holistic Side Note:** *If you don't have a GMB page yet, simply do a search for "Google My Business" and click on the link to get your free business listing on Google.*

Let's look at GMB from the page level to the post level ...

To begin, let's take a quick look at what a GMB listing looks like in search results.

The above screen shot is a GMB search result for one of Cuppa SEO's main keyword phrases. You've probably seen something like this before when you've searched on Google. The GMB listing often sits at the top of the page, ABOVE organic results, which means if someone finds a good result for their query in the GMB results, they may not even bother to scroll down to the organic results. This means your Google My Business listing is VERY important!

As you can see, Cuppa SEO ranks #1 in this GMB search result. To rank this high, you must have a well-optimized GMB listing as well as a website with SEO brewed into every nook and cranny. You also need to be publishing posts through GMB regularly.

If you're a local business, optimizing your GMB listing is a key factor in getting found in your neck of the woods. So let's get started with the optimization process …

USING SEO TO OPTIMIZE YOUR GMB INFO FIELDS

Your Info fields exist under the "Info" tab of your GMB listing. At first glance, these fields may seem mundane, but each and every one of them adds to the overall authority of your listing.

As of this writing, here's how you get to your Info page.

Log into GMB. Obvious, right? If you don't already have your login page bookmarked, here it is: https://www.google.com/business/.

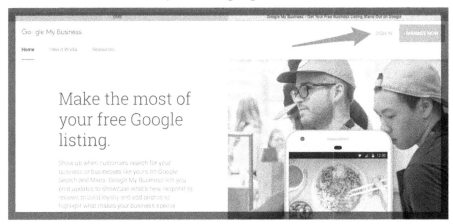

Your Google username and password should be the same for all your business-related Google accounts (Gmail, Google Docs, etc.). Once logged in, you should wind up on the Home page.

You can get to the Info page by clicking "Info" on the left-side navigation.

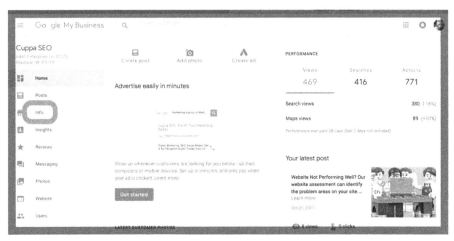

Once you arrive on the Info page, you can begin the optimization process.

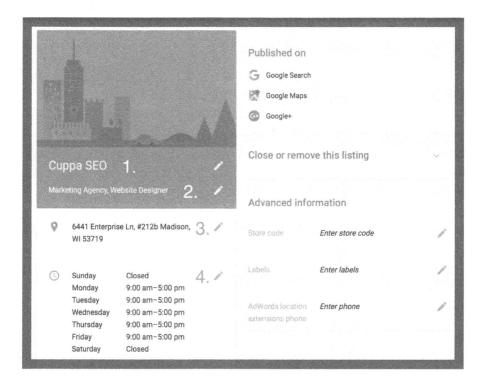

1. Your Business Name
Pretty straight forward, right? Be sure to enter your EXACT business name here. The same holds true for any online listing you use for your business, including Facebook, Twitter, LinkedIn, other local listings such as Yellow Pages, Foursquare, etc. Keeping your business name consistent across all online channels can improve your overall online authority.

2. Category
The next field after your business name is what's called a Category. This is where you define your business type based on a dropdown list provided by Google. Just start entering your business industry or business type, and Google will give you suggestions to choose from. Often, there won't be an exact match for your business type, so you need to choose the closest match. If possible, choose one or more secondary categories, too, as it helps define your business more clearly within your listing.

3. Address

An easy one, right? Well, maybe, if you have an actual business office or retail shop. If this is the case, enter your address here. Again, as with your company name, keep it consistent across all online channels. In other words, your address should be exactly the same on every single directory listing you have, social or otherwise. If it's not, you may lose authority points because of inconsistency.

If you work out of a home office, your address becomes more complicated. Why? Because it's typically not a good idea to represent your business as home-based. When you enter your home address into your Google My Business listing, Google will show an actual photo of your house!

This is bad for a couple of reasons. (1) It can cause a poor perception of your business because you "work from home." In other words, potential clients may perceive you as less professional, or less serious, than businesses with an actual business address. (2) You also don't want clients unexpectedly showing up on your doorstep.

In days past, the solution for home-based businesses was to open an account with a local UPS store for a business mailbox, which provides an actual, FULL address that can be used as your business address. But Google doesn't allow that anymore.

Holistic Side Note: A P.O. box won't do, and "hiding" your address within your Google My Business listing tends to severely hurt your chances of showing up at the top of a GMB search result.

What's a good solution if you work from home? You can join a local coworking space and request to use that physical address for your GMB listing. If you do this, be sure to ask for permission. Otherwise, you'll have to deal with your home address/house photo showing, or hide it and deal with the consequences.

After submitting your address to Google, you will receive a postcard with a verification PIN to complete the process. It typically arrives within a few days. Once you receive it, log into your GMB account, and you should see a prompt to enter the verification PIN.

4. Hours
Even if your hours vary, enter some standardized business hours for every day of the week.

If we scroll down a bit, we'll find more Info regions to populate ...

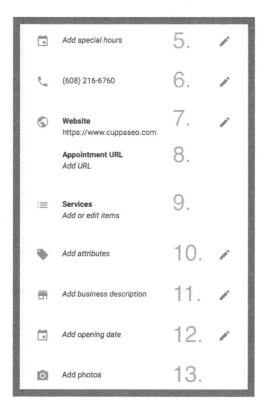

5. Special Hours
Populate this field only if you actually have special hours. A good example would be a retail shop that's open longer during the holiday season or announcing that you're closed on Thanksgiving.

6. Phone
Enter your main business phone here. It's OK if you're using a cell phone for your business.

7. Website URL

Enter the complete website address for your business including "http" or "https." Make sure the address you enter leads to your homepage.

8. Appointment URL

Like most of these regions, this one is pretty obvious. If you are a business that has online scheduling (as would a massage therapist or a hair stylist), you can insert the URL to your appointments page here. Depending on your type of business, you might be able to make other selections in your Info section such as placing an order or reserving a table.

9. Services

In this region you can add services, describe them, and price them ...

10. Add Attributes

According to Google, attributes tell customers more about your business (e.g. 'Has Wi-Fi,' 'Offers outdoor seating,' etc.). You can edit certain factual attributes (outdoor seating,for example), while subjective attributes (such as whether your business is popular with locals) rely on the opinions of Google users who have visited your business.

11. Add Business Description to Your "From the Business" Section

Like it or not, this is your new Story section where you can describe your business' products/services. When Google+ was still around, it had a Story section that allowed you to add over 3,000 characters of content to your GMB listing. That is gone, and it has been replaced with a "From the Business" section (kind of an awkward name, right?). The From the Business section gives you up to 750 characters, including spaces, to share a brief description about your business. When you populate this region, be sure to optimize it by using your keyword report to identify relevant product/service names that have some SEO value. Then give a brief description of each product/service (remember, you have only 750 CHARACTERS).

As an example, here's our current From the Business content:

> WEB DESIGN SERVICES
> Our holistic approach to web design means we build websites that get found, build trust & make it easy for visitors take the next step in becoming a customer. It's an approach that looks at your website as a whole — addressing all of the major success points — so it's a fully functioning site that helps you build your business.
>
> SEARCH ENGINE OPTIMIZATION (SEO)
> SEO is a strategy that helps increase relevant traffic to your website by improving your site's ranking in search results. In other words, SEO makes it easier for the people who are searching for what you offer to find you.
>
> ADWORDS MANAGEMENT
> We help clients experience higher conversion rates & a lower cost per click for a better return on investment.

This totals 735/750 characters, which is incredibly brief as compared with the old Story section in Google+.

12. Add an Opening Date
Enter the day, month and year your business opened.

13. Add Photos

Although the Add Photos section is under the GMB Info tab, we're going to cover it later in this section. This is only one of many ways to access it.

You might have noticed additional regions on the right side of the Info page. Depending on your business, some of them may have relevance, but we're not going to cover them here, as they're not SEO-centric.

GOOGLE MY BUSINESS: OPTIMIZING IMAGES
You've heard "A picture is worth a thousand words." But if you haven't properly named your images before uploading them into your GMB listing, they're worth nothing to Google.

That's why we're going to talk all about how to optimize your images before implementing them into your listing.

Let's start by getting you to the right place in GMB.

To start, go to your Home page. From there, click on the Photos tab in the left-hand nav.

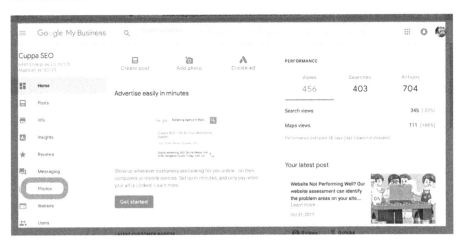

Once you've accessed your photos section, there are different regions where you can implement optimized images. But before we get into discussing each of these regions, let's first review how to actually optimize your GMB listing photos.

- Take out your keyword report. It's the foundation for optimizing every image you upload into Google My Business.
- Assess what your image is about. Let's go back to our dental office example and the image is about a root canal.

- The original image name is: "IMG_28651.jpg" which has no SEO value, or value to the human eye, whatsoever.
- You look at your keyword report and determine, "Root Canal Madison" is a good keyword phrase for this image.
- So you change the image name to, "Root-Canal-Madison.jpeg" or maybe you include your business name, too, "Caffeinated-Dentist-Root-Canal-Madison.jpeg" (fictitious, of course)
- Notice how I've structured the hierarchy of these image names, with each word being separated by a hyphen. There are NO spaces, and NO underscores — both of which would hurt the SEO value of the image.
- You'll have to optimize your image BEFORE you upload it to your Google My Business listing.
- When naming images, keep the length of the name at around 50 characters or fewer, including hyphens, as names that run too long can appear spammy.

Once all is said and done, you'll want to have at least 20–24 images (or more) optimized and uploaded into your listing.

Next, let's look at the regions that can be populated in your Photos section. There are a lot options, but be sure to add imagery to *at least* the first three I've listed ...

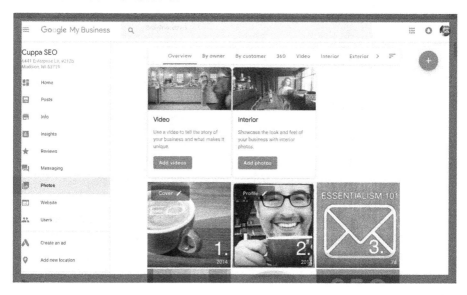

1. **Cover:** This is the large, rectangular photo that sits at the top of your GMB listing. Again, it should represent your brand identity well.

2. **Profile Photo:** This is a must. Be sure to put an image here that clearly identifies your brand. This can also be a photo of you.

3. **Overview:** Formerly called Additional Photos, this is a convenient place to add imagery/photos that don't quite fit into one of the more specific regions Google provides. It's also a good place to manually add the images you're using in your GMB posts. Sadly, GMB doesn't automatically add your post's imagery to Photos anymore.

Additional Photo tabs:

- **By Owner & By Customer:** These tabs will show you photos that were uploaded by the owner of the GMB page, or by a non-owner (customer).

- **360:** Exactly what it sounds like, this is a 360-degree view of your space. Google typically provides a 360-degree look at the outside of your building, but you can add more.

- **Video:** This is a nice spot to repurpose videos you've made for social media, webinars, presentations or your website. Google asks you to "tell the story behind your business and what makes it special." That said, I'm sticking with the strategy of posting video that is customer-centric as opposed to me-centric.

- **Interior:** If you have an establishment such as a retail shop, art gallery, coffee shop or any type of business where you might want to show off what's inside, the Interior Photos section is the place to do it.

- **Exterior:** These help potential visitors know what your establishment looks like from the outside. Or if your business is visual (maybe architecture or landscaping), this would be a great place to show off some photos.

- **At Work:** These can be of your people working on a project, or they can be other ways of showing the services or products you offer.

- **Team:** This section is dedicated to your coworkers! Make sure you get their permission before posting their photo.

- **Identity:** If you have a professional logo, upload it here. To access this tab, click the arrow on the right side of the navigation on your Photos page.

I hope this helps paint a clear picture (pun intended) on how to optimize the images and video you implement into your Google My Business listing!

GOOGLE MY BUSINESS: UPLOADING IMAGES

Now that you know how to optimize your images, and we've discussed where they go, let's walk through how to implement them into your GMB listing.

Once you're logged into GMB, click on the Photos tab in the left-side nav, just like we did in the previous example.

When you arrive on the Photos page, Google places you on the Overview tab. To upload your photos, click on the blue button in the upper right corner that has the plus sign in it. If you prefer to upload optimized imagery into a different section — maybe Interior or At Work — click on the appropriate tab first before clicking on the blue button.

Next, you'll see a pop-up window, like this:

If you're adding a batch of optimized images, you can highlight them all and drag them into this window. All the photos should upload at once. If Google has an issue with one or more of the images (usually it's that they're too small in size and won't render clearly if uploaded), it will let you know.

You can also drag one image in at a time or click on the blue button that allows you to "select photos from your computer," which will open up your file manager so you can drill down to where the image is stored.

Once you've dragged the photo in or selected it from a folder, Google will upload and save it automatically.

Now you're done!

CONVERSION AND USER EXPERIENCE IN YOUR GMB LISTING
When it comes to your GMB listing, there's virtually no wiggle room when it comes to how your page (or in this case your listing) is laid out. As we'll see, Facebook and LinkedIn offer more flexibility.

But that doesn't mean we should forgo examining conversion and user experience.

The User Experience
You can make the greatest impact on user experience by:

1. Ensuring that all of your information — hours of operation, address, phone number, website URL, etc. — are completely filled out and accurate. When someone is seeking information — your phone number, for example — it's right there.

2. Getting customer reviews! Ask customers — at least those who are overjoyed with you — to write a review on your Google My Business listing. In addition to helping boost the authority of your listing, it can also be beneficial to the user experience, because even a handful of good reviews helps people feel more *confident* and *comfortable* with using your services or buying your product.

Conversion
Once again, this is where providing good information comes in handy. Without it, people won't be able to take the next step with you. When someone is on your GMB listing, successful conversion includes:

1. A phone call
2. Having someone visit your establishment (if you're a retail shop)
3. A click-through to your website

There's one more thing that will aid in conversion or could even be considered a micro-conversion: **reviews.**

You might be thinking, "Again with the reviews?" Yes, because they're important. In the case of conversion, just as we mentioned above, if we can legitimately (and ethically) have people feeling more confident and comfortable with us, that means they're more likely to trust us. In turn, that makes it more likely that they WILL convert and become a customer.

14. SEO, UX and Conversion in Your GMB Posts

GOOGLE MY BUSINESS: PUBLISHING A POST

Before taking a look at how to apply SEO, UX and conversion into your posts, we'll take a look at how to publish a post through your Google My Business listing.

Once you're signed in, click on the Posts tab in the left-hand nav, and you'll see something like this ...

Prepare Your Post

See that blue circle with a square in it at the bottom right corner of the above image? Click on it to open a window and publish a post. You'll see something like this (Google regularly updates the look of this page):

At the top of this Create Post pop up, you'll notice a few things:
- "Preview" and "Publish" buttons, which are self explanatory.
- "What's New" is meant to be a newsy post, but it is also the best place to highlight your latest blog post.
- "Event," "Offer" and "Product" tabs are also very specific — and great if you happen to be promoting one of these items.

I've taken the liberty of populating the post so you can see what one looks like:
- We've got a short title, "Confused by Conversion?"
- Followed by brief copy.
- Along with a link back to the Cuppa SEO blog. Typically, I like to shorten the URL with Bitly or something similar, which is what I've done here. If the URL is too long, it can make the post "muddy," which is why a shortened URL is typically a better solution.
- In addition to using a URL in the content of your GMB post, you can also add a button that links to where you want to drive visitors. To do this, just scroll down a bit in the Create Post window and you'll

see a prompt to "Add a Button."

From here you can choose what you want the button to say ...

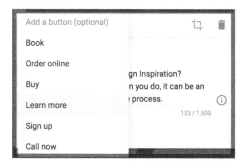

And drop in the destination URL ...

- For imagery, Google no longer does you the favor of inserting imagery that already exists on the page/blog post you are linking to, so you'll have to do it manually. Simply click on the blue camera in the image area and you'll be prompted to upload your pic ...

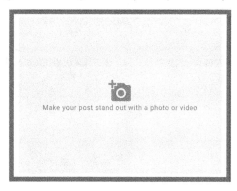

- Once you've double-checked your work, click on the "Publish" button, and your post will go live. Be sure to publish to "Public" unless you want to publish directly to a collection for a specific reason.

Holistic Side Note: There's one more thing you need to do before you're done here. Go to the Photos section of your Google My Business listing and upload the same image you used here into your Photos collection. It will add a little more SEO juice to your Google My Business listing.

What All This Looks Like

You might be wondering where your post goes and what it looks like after you publish. It shows up in your Google My Business listing, and can be seen when someone searches for your business, like this ...

I've searched Google for Cuppa SEO. This is what you see at the top of the results (organic results are on the left, GMB listing is on the right) ...

Scrolling down toward the bottom of the GMB listing reveals my most recent post (still on the right) ...

And if you click on it, you see the full post ...

In addition to a post appearing in your GMB listing, if Google deems your post newsy or important enough — it can also appear in natural search results.

Holistic Side Note: A published post on GMB stays "live" for a week before it expires. Before this happens, you should receive an email from Google that states: "Notice: Your post is about to expire. Your previous post is about to disappear from your Business Profile. Create a new post with special deals, news or updates to make your business stand out."

It's important to note that expired posts still exist, they just don't show in the listing. Here's what it looks like after a post has expired from the Cuppa SEO listing ...

When someone clicks on "View previous posts on Google," all previous posts can be viewed.

SEO, UX AND CONVERSION IN GMB POSTS

Let's take a moment to dissect a well-optimized GMB post, covering all three disciplines as we go along.

Title
Online Marketing Consulting

SEO: Here, the entire title is a relevant keyword phrase with SEO value. The only downside is that the title is a bit bland, but in this particular case (one of many tests for our consulting services), SEO value trumped "romance."

UX: That being said, the title is short, clear and easy to understand, so the reader doesn't have to think about it, which makes for a positive user experience. Any ambiguity is paid off by both the imagery, and the sentence that sits below the title.

Conversion: As you may have guessed, conversion doesn't come directly into play in the title. BUT, if the title didn't have a good UX — say it was really long or ambiguous — you'd have less chance of someone reviewing the rest of the post and clicking on your link. That's why I consider the title a "soft conversion," or a conversion leader.

Brief Content
Under our Title, the copy reads: *Provides your team with a solid understanding of SEO, UX & Conversion as well as how to apply these disciplines into your website, blog & social media. https://goo.gl/Q0FK3l*

SEO: The copy has some relevant supportive keywords, which is ideal ... but it's a good reminder to always write your posts for the *reader first!* In other words, your content (and your title for that matter) may not always be optimized with keywords. If this is the case, it's OK — as long as it's a choice and not an oversight.

UX: Most important, it plays off the title and adds clarification, which is good for the UX. It's also on the short side (and has been streamlined even further since I published this post), which also provides a better UX. The shorter, the better. Remember: Copy in your GMB post is an appetizer — not a main course. It should be as clear, as engaging and *as short* as possible. If someone has to "click for more," it probably means your post content is too long.

Conversion: Conversion now comes directly into play with the text link at the end of the copy. This leads to one of two places (depending on what our intention is): (1) our Online Marketing Consulting web page that contains a lot more info; or (2) our squeeze page for this consulting service, which contains just enough info to engage with visitors and (hopefully) have them contact us to discuss things further.

Either way, the point is to make sure you've got a link, or a button, in the GMB post leading to YOUR website, squeeze page or blog. If you drive traffic to someone else's content, your conversion strategy has gone awry!

Imagery
The last item we're going to talk about here is your imagery, which is a critical component to your GMB post.

SEO: An optimized image makes your post easier to find on social media and in organic searches, so be sure to optimize your imagery as we outlined earlier.

UX: The picture is your instant UX meter; it provides a positive, negative or neutral experience in the blink of an eye. If the image doesn't cause a positive UX, there's less of a chance for engagement.

When your picture relates to your headline and copy, its UX value goes up even further. With a cohesive post, I don't have to think about how the copy and the picture go together, because it's obvious.

Conversion: Clicking on your GMB post image no longer leads anywhere (like it used to on Google+), so there's no direct conversion associated with clicking on the image. That said, an engaging image that supports your message is still part of the conversion process because it adds to an improved UX, which in turn can make visitors more likely to click on your link or button.

15. Facebook Business Page

Now that we've tackled Google My Business, let's take a look at Facebook — specifically your business page.

Before we begin, it's important to note that you need to have a personal Facebook account in order to create a Facebook Business page. The good thing, though, is that more than one person can be given permission to manage that business page.

A Facebook Business page is most effective for businesses and organizations that have a business to consumer (B2C) model. In other words, the business or organization sells to an individual. Good examples of this would be a running shoe company (local or national), or a local hairdresser. For a business like Cuppa SEO, Facebook isn't the best place to try to gain customers, because we're business to business (B2B). It's an important distinction to make early in your social media journey, because you want to apply your resources (both time and money) where you can expect the greatest ROI.

That being said, it's time to take a look at how to add a healthy dose of SEO, UX and conversion to your Facebook Business page and to your Facebook Business posts. We'll also look at Facebook Live and take a quick peek at a feature called Boost Post (which can connect you with people you DON'T know). Boost Post is a paid service, which is why we'll talk about it only briefly so you know that it exists. As with the rest of the book, we're not covering paid advertising options.

USING SEO TO OPTIMIZE YOUR FACEBOOK BUSINESS PAGE
Although Google My Business holds the lion's share of social media SEO value, it's still a good idea to take a close look at SEO, UX and CV on your other social media channels — including Facebook.

Optimizing Your Info Fields
The first thing you need to do is get to your Facebook Business page. If you don't have one set up, go here to get started: https://www.facebook.com/pages/create/. You'll be prompted to log into your personal account, if you aren't already.

If you do have a Facebook Business page, the easiest way to get there is by first going to your *personal Facebook page*, which you probably frequent daily (this is all easier to do from a computer as opposed to a mobile device).

Once on your personal Facebook page, take a look at the left-hand navigation. There, you'll be able to access your business page (or pages) through "Shortcuts" or by clicking on the "Pages" button.

Next, you'll see your actual page. When you get there, the first thing you'll want to do is to implement *optimized images* to the top of the page.

Profile Pic

This is the square image in the upper left-hand corner. It can be your company logo or an image of you if you are an integral part of your company's brand.

Cover Photo

This is the large, hero image that lives at the top of your page. As you can see, mine is a coffee cup (big surprise).

Next, you'll want to direct your attention back to the left-hand nav ...

This navigation will bring you to all the sections you need to optimize. Remember, all we're focusing on here is optimizing key areas of your Facebook Business page. Let's start off with ...

Services

Often overlooked, the Services tab in the left-hand navigation brings you to a page where you can add one or more services to your Facebook Business page.

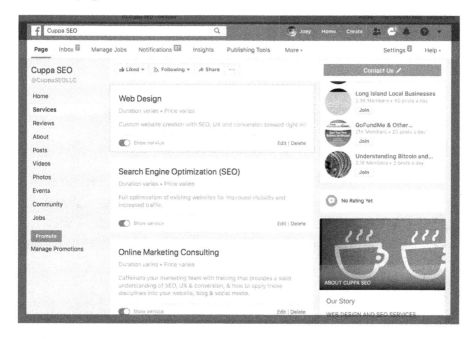

Simply click on "Add a Service" to populate a new service listing, or click on the Edit link in an existing service to edit.

Although there isn't room for a ton of information, you can add: (1) a service name, (2) price (if applicable), (3) a brief description, (4) and an image. Make sure your service name and description are clear and contain at least one keyword phrase, if possible. And of course if you use an image, make sure it's optimized!

The Services area helps define who you are within your Facebook Business page, making it easier for the internal algorithm to identify you for the services you offer.

About

There are a lot of items, large and small, to tackle within the About section. The good news: Most of the optimized information and content you created for your Google My Business page can be used here.

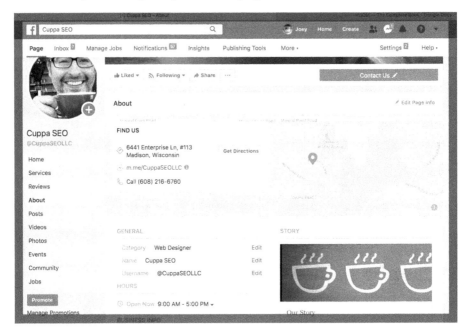

Find Us

If you click on "Edit Page Info" (to the right in the About banner), you'll be able to add/edit your address, direct link to Facebook Messenger, and your Facebook Business username. Make sure all are accurate and that the address here is *identical* to what you have on your GMB listing.

General

Here, we'll begin our work with the General section (just below the "Find Us" box).

- *Category:* choose one or more relevant categories that define your business. In some cases, you'll find one or more direct matches. In other cases, you will have to choose the category that best matches what you do. In my case, my categories are *web designer* and *marketing consultant.* There are no *SEO* or *web design*-related phrases.

- *Name:* populate this region with the actual name of your business.
- *Username:* This is your Facebook username for the business page. It can be customized, but if somebody has already claimed a username, you won't be able to use it.

Hours

This one's pretty self-explanatory. Enter your business hours here. And if your business hours are a little unpredictable or driven by customer demand, that's OK. Just enter the times you generally work as accurately as possible. Also, if you're a retail shop and you're closed on Mondays, make sure it's reflected here. You don't want someone showing up when you're closed!

Story

To the right of the General section, you'll find the Story section.

Remember the Business Description section on your Google My Business page? The Facebook Story section serves the same purpose, which is to provide visitors AND Facebook with specifics about your business and the services/products you provide. My recommendation: Simply add to your Google My Business Business Description and place it here.

I say "add to," because Facebook allows quite a bit more characters than Google does for their Business Description section. My Facebook Story is 2,891 characters long, and I've tested up to 3,000 characters, which is more than enough to provide good, relevant, *optimized* content.

When you add additional content, you're also freshening it a bit. The content in your Facebook Story can be identical to your Google My Business Story, but it helps to modify it so it's not identical — and why not take advantage of all those extra characters Facebook allows?

Although there's no need to worry about duplicate content here, it's just the process I've developed over the years. What happens is, Google sees the first iteration of the content as the original, and the copy as syndication. The original gets the authority/SEO value, and the syndicated content gets none.

If you plan on using the same Story on multiple social media platforms, I strongly advise optimizing your entire GMB page before optimizing any other social media platforms. Google will perceive your GMB content as the original — ensuring that it doesn't lose any authority or SEO value by being perceived as syndication. And that's important if you want to ensure that your GMB Business Description ranks well (why wouldn't you?) in the Google My Business section of search results (which we talked about earlier).

To a degree, this is a precautionary measure, as I can't find hard data from Google on the subject of Google My Business and syndication. The best information I have to go on is based on the process we've implemented for dozens of clients — and it works.

Here's my complete Facebook Business Story as an example of what optimized content could look like …

> WEB DESIGN AND SEO SERVICES
> Cuppa SEO creates websites with search engine optimization, user experience and conversion brewed right in.
>
> What that means, in plain English, is that we build websites that get found, build trust, and make it easy for visitors take the next step in becoming a customer.
>
> WEB DESIGN
> We start with a site design that's customized to your company's personality, goals and needs. You won't find cookie-cutter designs here, just fantastic, beautiful design that engages with visitors from the moment they arrive on your site.
>
> Our web designers build sites in Wordpress, Drupal & Expression Engine. Every site we build is optimized with SEO baked into every nook and cranny, plus we make them mobile friendly, too. In addition to creating great-looking sites, we also make sure they have solid user experience & conversion strategies in place.
>
> SEARCH ENGINE OPTIMIZATION (SEO)
> SEO services include in-depth research of your industry and the creation of a comprehensive list of optimal keyword phrases that can be implemented into your website, blog and social media campaigns.

Successful SEO includes implementing these keyword phrases into critical areas such as title tags, alternate image tags, headlines and page content to improve your visibility with search engines. The result is more traffic on your website, and with more traffic comes the potential to increase your revenue.

USER EXPERIENCE (UX)
Once our SEO efforts bring more traffic to your site, UX comes into play. User experience is exactly what is sounds like — the positive, negative or indifferent experience viewers have when they visit your site. Our web design process ensures that your UX is positive, helping visitors to immediately feel comfortable when they arrive on your site. We also make sure that all content, imagery and calls-to-action are easy to digest — without having to think about it. This adds up to a pleasant experience that helps build trust.

CONVERSION
Now that we have visitors feeling good about where they've arrived, we need a solid conversion strategy to ensure they know exactly what to do next. Whether it's filling out a contact form, giving you a call, or downloading some complimentary content, our conversion strategies make next steps crystal clear.

BLOGGING
Whether you're a business connecting with customers and building brand awareness or an individual talking with your audience, a blog is an effective way to communicate and build relationships. A blog can go a long way toward making you a trusted, relevant resource. It has the ability to improve engagement and overall reach — plus it's a perfect medium to express yourself, be heard and help others.

Cuppa SEO offers customizable blogging packages to meet your needs — and your budget. Every blog post is optimized for search engines and for the human eye.

Please feel free to contact Cuppa SEO with questions or for more details!

Now, let's check out the bottom half of the About section ... don't worry, we're almost done ...

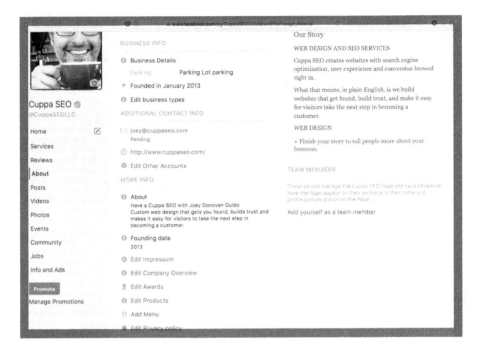

Business Info

In this small section, there are two regions to populate ...

Business details (edit business details)

Here, you can choose a price range to show overall cost as well as parking details (street, parking lot, valet).

When you click on Edit in the Business Details section (it appears when you hover over it), you'll be able to affect all of these items ...

Edit your details   ✕

BUSINESS

Price Range   ○ $
                 ○ $$
                 ○ $$$
                 ○ $$$$
                 ● **Unspecified**

Parking   ☐ Street   ☐ Valet
                 ☑ **Parking Lot**

See All Information

Price

If you own an establishment like a restaurant or bar, it's important to populate price so potential customers have a clear idea of cost before they arrive. With services such as web design, graphic design or art, you might want to leave price unspecified, as there are too many variables to consider (many often unknown to the visitor) to accurately predict price level.

For instance, pretty much anywhere you go, $20 is expensive for a shot of bourbon. Bourbon is a single-element product. It's a glass of deliciousness that you drink. But what about web design? Is it a Wordpress, Drupal or HTML site? How many pages? Is there a database? Custom build, or cookie cutter? You get the idea (BTW — stay away from cookie cutter websites, unless you want to be perceived as part of a really large crowd ...)

Parking

Convenient parking in Madison, Wisconsin, usually is pretty easy to find. But downtown? It's a pain. Let your potential visitors know what they can expect for your location. A parking lot in a busy city immediately makes your establishment more appealing (keep this fact in mind on your website, too!).

Start date (edit start date)

When was your business founded? Enter that info here. Facebook will let you enter the year, month — and even the day — your business began.

Edit Business Types
This region gives you a couple of additional business definers, if you need them.

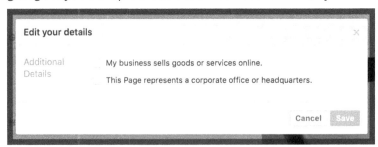

Additional Contact Info
This section is pretty simple. Enter your BUSINESS email address, and your website URL (if you have one). If you have other Facebook Business accounts, you can access (or add) them here.

> **Holistic Side Note:** *There are different schools of thought when it comes to one's email address. Many small businesses choose to have an "@gmail.com" address for various reasons. If you go this route, just keep in mind that you may not be perceived as serious or professional, because a free Gmail account does not evoke professionalism or success. It connotes cheap (it is free, after all) and can create doubt as to your credibility as a business. If you work for Nike, your email address had better be JoeyDG@Nike.com, not JoeyDG@Gmail.com.*

More Info
The More Info fields are ...

About
The About section in your About section (confusing, right?) is limited to 255 characters. It should be a high-level snapshot of what you do. Make it crystal clear, concise, and be sure to share at least one major benefit of doing business with you instead of a competitor. And remember: The more a benefit addresses the reason why someone typically buys* what you're selling, the better chance you have of engaging with that person emotionally.

Founding date
Be sure to populate this field accurately, as it can be a confidence booster (which is a form of optimizing your brand in the eyes of others) when a viewer sees you've been in business for 5, 10 or 20 years! Why Facebook makes us enter the founding date here *AND* in the Business Info section we talked about earlier is beyond me.

Edit Impressum
According to Facebook, "This is an optional field. In certain countries, such as Austria, Germany and Switzerland, businesses may be required by law to include a statement of ownership on their web presence. The limit is 2,000 characters."

Company Overview
You can populate this section with at least 3,000 characters, so it's pretty robust. But this one has me scratching my head, because at first glance it appears to be asking for the same info as the Story section. When I did a little research, I could see how this section is a bit different. A company overview is defined as, "an essential part of a business plan that overviews the most important points about your company ... history, leadership team, location, mission statement, etc.," giving this a more factual take than the Story section. Honestly, it's a bit ambiguous and confusing.

Here's how I addressed it: Instead of repeating the same info that I used for the Our Story section, I pulled some of the content off of my website's About page, which aligns with the definition mentioned above.

Edit Awards
If you've got 'em, flaunt 'em here.

Products
If your company is products based, this is the place to list your wares.

Add Menu

If you are a restaurant or bar, add your full menu here. Be sure to check to see how the menu appears to viewers. If there are quirks with spacing or characters, fix them!

OPTIMIZING IMAGES ON YOUR FACEBOOK BUSINESS PAGE

When it comes to optimizing images, the process is identical to what we talked about in the Google My Business section, so be sure to optimize your Facebook images in the same way. In fact, once you've optimized your imagery for any of your social media platforms (or for a blog post or web page), it should be good to go.

Uploading Images

Just as with Google My Business, you can upload images into the Photos section of your Facebook Business page. Click on Photos in the nav on the left, and here's what you'll see:

Albums

For some businesses, albums can be a great way to organize photos. Let's say your business takes people on hiking expeditions. Adding photos from each expedition as its own Album is a great way to keep things organized. It also can show viewers what expeditions look like at different times of the year — or at different destinations.

To add photos to a new album or albums, simply click on Create Album on the left side of the Albums section.

In Cuppa SEO's case, the bulk of our photos come from our posts and are not placed in any particular album. They all live in ...

All Photos

The All Photos section houses every single image you've ever uploaded into your Facebook Business page. You can Add Photos if you like, which is especially helpful if you're just starting your page.

Depending on your business type, this can be an easy or a difficult task. For example, one of our clients, ZenDogz, is an enlightened daycare facility for dogs. Boy, do they have a lot of photos of happy pups! But if you're a consulting agency, you might not have more than a handful of photos to share (if that), because all you have is team photos and your logo.

If the latter is the case for you, no worries! Over time as you publish relevant content *with imagery* in your posts, your images will be added to your All Photos section.

If you do have images to add, simply click on the Add Photos button on the upper right side of the All Photos section.

Whether it's in Albums or All Photos, be sure you optimize your images before uploading to your Facebook Business page.

16. UX and Conversion in Your Facebook Business Page

Moving on from SEO, let's look at some ways you can positively affect UX and conversion on your Facebook Business page.

CREATING A SOLID USER EXPERIENCE
The more thoroughly you populate your Facebook Business page with accurate, relevant, benefit-driven customer-centric content and imagery, the better the user experience will be.

When visitors arrive on your Facebook Business page, you want them to see original imagery on your Home tab (if at all possible) that represents the essence of who you are as a business (no cheesy stock photos!). Choose engaging imagery that makes people feel at home and comfortable (this helps build trust), instead of imagery that is devoid of humanity.

Taking time to ensure that the content on your Services and About sections is consistent, clear and customer-centric will go a long way toward boosting viewer engagement. The result? Better UX.

If you're not quite sure if your imagery and content fit these criteria, ASK some of your customers, colleagues or trusted friends (who will not just placate you) what they think. After all, your Facebook Business page — like anything else in online marketing, business and life — is a test. The more you test, the more accurately you can determine whether something works, kind of works or is a complete dud. Without intentional testing and recalculation, how can you ever expect to improve?

Whether or not you can help someone's organization is typically not the first question a visitor will ask. Some of the first questions (posed consciously or subconsciously) will be, "Do I like these people ... and do I trust them?" If the answer to these is no, why would they want your help? The UX you offer on your social media platforms is critical to the overall success of your online marketing and the health of your brand.

UX and Your Facebook Business Page Hierarchy

Facebook understands that every business is different. That's why it gives us choices about where each of our Facebook Business page elements (like Posts, Videos, Photos, etc.) show up when a visitor stops by.

To edit your page hierarchy and aesthetic, simply go to Settings, and click on Templates and Tabs in the nav on the left.

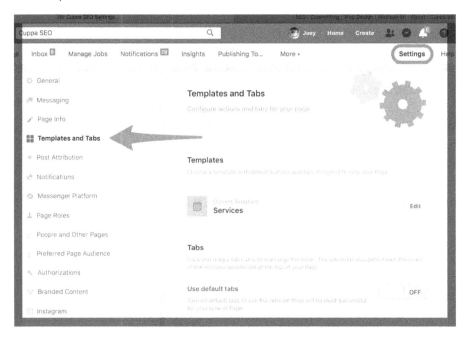

You can choose from templates built for Services, Business, Venues and more. It will take a little time to determine which of these templates is best for your business. Once you do, you'll next determine the best order for your Tabs and if there are any you want to delete.

For instance, I currently use the Services template, but I needed to turn off

"Use default tabs" (near the bottom of our Templates and Tabs example) so I could reorder the tabs for a better UX AND remove Tabs like "Shop" and "Offers," as they're not relevant for my business at this time. Because this book is in your hands (or on your electronic device), this has probably changed, because I'm going to want my visitors to buy my book! The ability to customize my Facebook Business page is an opportunity to ensure the best user experience possible for the visitor.

CONVERSION ON YOUR FACEBOOK BUSINESS PAGE

With a solid UX in place, you increase your chances for conversion in two ways:

First, an attractive UX means visitors are more likely to stick around. And the more they stick around, the better the possibility they will check out one of your posts and maybe click on whatever call-to-action it includes. We'll look at this later when we talk about Facebook Business posts.

Second, and directly relevant to your Facebook Business *page*, is the call-to-action button Facebook makes available. Here's what mine looks like ...

In addition to Contact Us, Facebook gives you a handful of categories and options to suit your business type. If don't have a button where you see Contact Us in the above screenshot, you should see a prompt from Facebook in that same region to create one. If you DO have an existing button, just hover over it to reveal a handful of options, including Edit.

Click on Edit to reveal the following ...

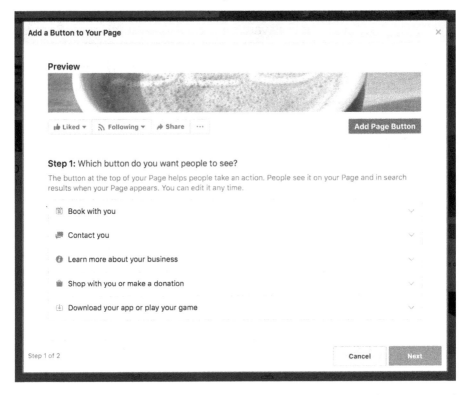

Each of the top-level categories gives you options on button language and where the button link takes you. When your button has been live for a few months, you can check analytics to see how many people have clicked on it. If your conversion rate is low or nonexistent, you can change the language/ intention of the button as well as where it leads to.

Here's an example of the options that live under the Contact category:

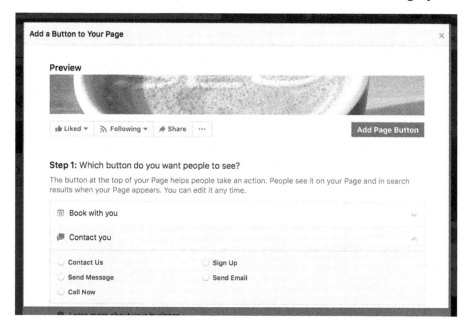

Just as we discussed with your website conversion, your conversion strategy here is to have visitors take the next step YOU want them to take. So choose wisely ...

17. SEO, UX and Conversion in Your Facebook Posts

PUBLISHING A POST

In stark contrast to publishing a post on Google My Business, publishing a post on Facebook is a breeze (accompanied by a cup of iced coffee, of course).

Let's walk through it quickly in case you haven't done it before ...

1. Go to your Facebook Business page, and you should see a region that says "Write a post."

2. Click in that region, and it will expand, allowing you to add your headline, content, text link (if you're looking to drive visitors to your website or blog), and photo or video. You'll also find many other options that may or may not be helpful (it's not the best UX) ...

SEO, UX AND CONVERSION

Here's an example of what a well-constructed Facebook Business post looks like ...

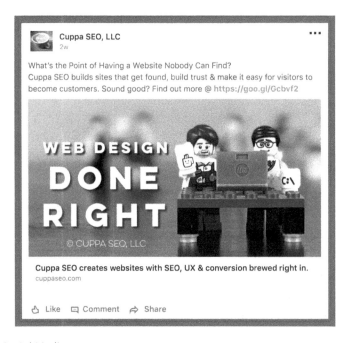

Title (Headline)

What's the Point of Having a Website Nobody Can Find?

We've got a clear, emotionally engaging title that is meant to connect with all of those who are frustrated with their website because it's not getting found — in other words, with someone who's not getting enough traffic on his or her website.

SEO: Whenever possible, I like to include a keyword phrase in the title of my Facebook Business posts. As you can see, this is NOT the case here. I always like to say, "Never sacrifice the quality of your content for the sake of SEO. Search engine optimization needs to *support* your content, not weaken it."

Here, the emotional engagement I was looking for was paramount, which goes to show there is no one-size-fits-all solution for social media (or anything else, for that matter). You always need to take a moment to think about what your intention (or goal) is for every single Facebook Business post you publish, and then you need to follow through on that intention.

UX: The title is clear, especially to those who are having problems with their website traffic — and these are the folks we want to connect with. The title also offers a good UX to this demographic, because it shows understanding of a serious problem someone is experiencing. If the person reading the post fits into this category, that individual might be feeling hurt (even betrayed) by a previous web developer who charged a premium price for a subpar website that isn't performing.

The title is further clarified/supported by the brief copy that follows it as well as the imagery that contains the message "Web Design Done Right."

Conversion: As you might have guessed, conversion doesn't come directly into play in the title. BUT if the title didn't have a good UX — say it was really long, ambiguous or didn't have an emotional tug — you'd have less chance of someone reviewing the rest of the post and clicking on your link. That's why I consider the title a "soft conversion," or a conversion leader.

Brief Content

Under our headline, the copy reads:

> Cuppa SEO builds sites that get found, build trust and make it easy for visitors to become customers. Sound good? Find out more @ https://goo.gl/J9M9wC

SEO: Except for "SEO" our copy doesn't have keywords in it. And that's OK, because once again, I am trying to engage with readers on an emotional level — and connect in terms they understand. So if you're wondering why my example isn't chock-full of keywords, that's why. Your Facebook Business post content (and title, for that matter) might not always be optimized with keywords. If this is the case, it's OK — as long as it's a choice and not an oversight.

I've done a lot of testing and research, and I've found that even my marketing-savvy clients don't respond well to words like "SEO," "user experience" and "conversion." They respond well to knowing I understand their problem and that I know how to solve it! That's why the copy here offers solutions to the problem that is addressed in the title.

UX: As you might have guessed, this content is good for UX, as it "pays off" the title and adds clarification. It's also on the short side, providing a solid UX. The shorter the better — as long as you're not sacrificing a clear, engaging message for brevity. As we mentioned in the Google My Business section, the content in your post is an appetizer, not a main course. It's meant to entice and engage readers so they are eager to take the next step, which of course is ...

Conversion: Once readers have taken the time to read our title and copy, we've got to give them a clear, easy path to taking the next step we want them to take. In this case, it's visiting Cuppa SEO's web design page.

In the example above, we've accomplished this with a shortened text link. We shortened it because we don't want it adding too much length to the page. Note: since Google URL Shortener no longer exists, I suggest using Bitly. That said, if the link to your web page or blog is short, feel free to use it — as long as it doesn't cause your post to truncate!

Imagery
At last, we've arrived at imagery, a critical component to any social media post — including your Facebook Business posts.

SEO: As you might have guessed, this image is well optimized. The actual image name is: Cuppa-SEO-Madison-WI-Web-Design-UX-Services.jpg.

As discussed earlier, an optimized image makes your post easier to find on social media and in organic searches. Believe it or not, I have seen some of my optimized Facebook posts show up on page one of an organic search. So be sure to optimize your imagery as we outlined earlier.

UX: Your picture/imagery is what I like to call your "stopper," because it can literally stop searchers in their tracks while they're scrolling through their Facebook feed. The picture is your instant UX meter, providing a positive, negative or neutral experience in the blink of an eye. If the image doesn't cause a positive UX, the scrolling continues (which is why choosing or creating engaging imagery is so important).

Your imagery should always support your post's headline and copy. When it does, the overall UX of your post rises. It's all about creating a cohesive post so the reader doesn't have to think about how the copy and the picture go together. It should be obvious.

What I find interesting is that the Lego characters in the "Web Design Done Right" image have tested very well with people. We did a photo shoot with them (they were very professional) to see how people would respond to them in our marketing materials — and they have been a big hit! They make a great stopper (as opposed to yet another selfie or stock photo), and they're kind of fun.

Conversion: If at all possible, make sure your imagery is clickable AND that it leads to the content you're highlighting in your post. For example, when clicked, the imagery in our current example leads the reader directly to our Web Design page. But this does not happen by chance, so let's discuss the process ...

To have the imagery in my Facebook Business post link directly to my Web Design page, the image first needs to live on my actual Web Design page. In other words, when I created the page, I needed to think ahead and use imagery that would also look good on social media. It needed to be sized correctly (so it fit well in within the parameters of my Facebook Business post) and have a clear message that made sense on my site as well as on social channels.

Once the imagery is on my Web Design page, when I add the link (or shortened link) to my Web Design page into my Facebook Business post, Facebook automatically pulls the image into the post. Even better, that image is coded (by Facebook) to be a direct link to my Web Design page!

Now my image and my text link both drive people to the same place — which is a big plus for conversion (and for UX, too).

On the other hand, if you upload an image directly into your Facebook Business post (from somewhere like your desktop, Dropbox account or photo library), when clicked it won't lead people to where you want them to go. Instead, it will only make the image bigger — which means you'll potentially lose out on converting someone. Avoid this. Take the time to set things up right if it's possible to do so.

Holistic Side Note: *The copy you see directly below the image in our example ...*

"Web Design Madison WI | SEO | UX | Web Design Services | Cuppa SEO"

... is also automatically imported by Facebook. If you're wondering where it came from, it's the title tag for my Web Design page (we talked about title tags back in the SEO section of the book).

Facebook also pulled in the meta description for our Web Design page, but I deleted it because it was distracting. To edit content in the region below the image, click in it before you publish the post.

Holistic Side Note: *Really, Joey? Another Holistic Side Note so soon? Yes, indeed ...*

- *For greater reach, be sure to publish your post to the public.*

- *When you publish a post (either before or after it's published), you might notice a "Boost Post" button toward the lower right side of your post. Boosting a post is a way to disseminate your message to people who are not in your circle of Facebook connections. In other words, you can target Facebook users by region, age, hobby, etc. But because we're not talking about paid marketing/advertising strategies in this book, I will leave it at this — if you're a B2C business, you'll want to strongly consider becoming familiar with how to boost a post on your Facebook Business page.*

18. Facebook Live

Have you seen a Facebook Live event? As you might already know, it's a video that's recorded live on Facebook ... and I know exactly what most of you are thinking: You want to run for the hills because most of you have no interest in going live on Facebook!

But wait, don't run! Instead, hear me out (and afterward, you still shouldn't run).

I love to talk — and I love to present — but I was hesitant to try Facebook Live when it was new. The biggest reasons for this were:

(1) You could only go live from your mobile phone. This is no longer true, as now you can broadcast on Chrome or Firefox right from your desktop. In fact, there's even third-party software that allows you to show multiple screens on Facebook Live so you can facilitate webinars just like you would on a dedicated webinar platform.

(2) Much of what I was seeing broadcast was less than impressive (for various reasons I won't go into). Then I had to remind myself that there's always a lot of bad content out there. In this case, it's just in video form. I decided not to use other people's bad content as an excuse — because I realized all I had to do was deliver relevant, helpful content just like I would in a blog post, webinar or workshop.

(3) I wanted my videos to look professional, and I didn't have much video equipment. Another easy fix. A quick search on Amazon and I had a

workable lighting set for under forty bucks. I already had a professional-grade tripod with phone attachment, but if you don't have one, they're available on Amazon for under fifteen bucks. So to look professional, it will cost you about $50, assuming you have a clean shirt and a brush to comb your hair. A professional-looking video is important because if you look amateur, you'll be perceived as amateur — which will not evoke confidence in your products or services.

(4) Prep time. You've got to set everything up, decide what you're going to talk about, for how long — and then actually do it! Even a five-minute Facebook Live event could take you 1–2 hours to do it right.

But people like video. Test after test shows that people prefer to watch stuff as opposed to reading it. In other words, video can be more engaging — as long as it's good content.

EXAMINING A FACEBOOK LIVE EVENT
Notice that I refer to Facebook Live as an event. For all intents and purposes, it *is* an event, although you might have only a handful of people who watch it live. Let's examine what goes into creating a successful broadcast:

- Select relevant, helpful content just as you do with all content you create.

- Pick your topic ahead of time, make some notes, and do a couple of run-throughs.

- Decide how long the broadcast is going to be BEFORE your start.

  - I prefer brief broadcasts, which generally get watched AFTER the live version is over.
  - If you do a longer broadcast, you have a better chance of engaging with people while you're live — but it's harder to keep people around for 20 minutes or more unless you're delivering fantastic content. You might want to test this by facilitating a webinar or longer piece of content on Facebook Live, and then review your analytics to see how many people engaged and for how long they stuck around.

- Set up all of your equipment at least 30 minutes before broadcasting, and test to make sure it's working properly.

If you are a personable speaker, and you're able to express your expertise in a way just about anybody can understand, you will probably be very successful with Facebook Live. If you are not an experienced speaker, or if you feel overwhelmed by this whole process, consider joining Toastmasters or facilitating workshops at small, local networking events. Have someone film you and analyze your presentation afterward. And be sure to ask for feedback, as we can often be our own harshest critic!

A FACEBOOK LIVE EXAMPLE BROADCAST

The first Facebook Live event I broadcast was 2.5 minutes long, reached 502 people, and received 190 views. And I didn't spend a dime on it. I was floored by these results, as a typical non-video post reaches 100–150 viewers, at best. Such is the power of video.

To begin a Facebook Live event, go to your Facebook Business page and click on the Live button …

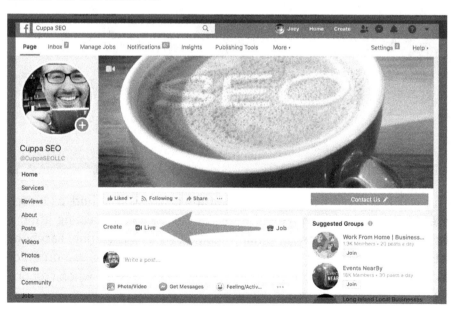

After that you'll receive some brief instructions, and you're off!

Here's a screenshot of a broadcast ...

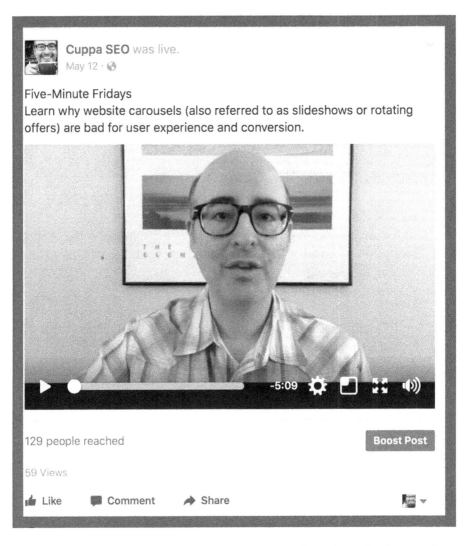

Cuppa SEO was live.
May 12 · 🌐

Five-Minute Fridays
Learn why website carousels (also referred to as slideshows or rotating
offers) are bad for user experience and conversion.

-5:09 ⚙ 🔲 ⛶ 🔊

129 people reached   Boost Post

59 Views

👍 Like   💬 Comment   ➤ Share

This was broadcast from my computer, my preferred method, as I often
like to show visual examples of what I'm talking about, treating it more
like a multi-camera event or a mini-webinar. As of this writing, Facebook
lets you broadcast only from your camera (on your phone, computer, or
a camera attached to your computer), which is a challenge when creating
multi-camera or multi-screen events.

That said, there are third-party applications that help you do just that. The one I typically use is OBS (https://obsproject.com), which is free. It is effective, but the user experience is a bit clunky. If you decide to use it, be sure to do a practice run or two before your live broadcast.

Believe it or not, we've reached the end of our Facebook Business section. Now let's move on to everyone's favorite B2B social media platform, LinkedIn ...

19. LinkedIn Company Page

Welcome to the LinkedIn section of the book. This is where we'll dive into the specifics of your LinkedIn Company page. But first, let's take a step back so you know exactly what to expect.

In order to "play" on LinkedIn, you need what's called a Personal Profile. This is a page where you "talk" about yourself professionally: where you've worked, skills, group and association affiliations, etc. You can also publish posts and connect with other professionals. Your Personal Profile also should be optimized, so it's good idea to review your profile and apply what you've learned throughout the book.

I won't discuss your Personal Profile beyond these basics. I'll instead focus on your LinkedIn Company Page.

If you don't already have a LinkedIn Company page, the easiest way to create one is to log into your Personal Profile, click on the Work icon in the upper right corner, scroll down in the side window that appears, and click "Create a Company Page." Then follow the onscreen instructions AFTER you've completed the LinkedIn section of this book so your SEO, UX and CV strategies are all in place right from the get-go.

As you likely have guessed, we're going to examine how to add SEO, UX and conversion to your LinkedIn Company page, and then we'll take a look at how to apply these three disciplines into every post you publish on your Company page. As we did with Facebook, we will touch on a paid service here — Sponsored Updates. (I know, I'm breaking my own rule about not discussing paid services, but I need to make sure you at least know about Sponsored Updates because it's super important — and nobody seems to know about it!)

Unlike Facebook, LinkedIn is a B2B-centric social media platform. So if you're like Cuppa SEO and do business only with other businesses and organizations, this is the place to be. But just because it's a B2B platform doesn't mean you should change your strategy of delivering solid, relevant, problem-solving content.

USING SEO TO OPTIMIZE YOUR LINKEDIN COMPANY PAGE
Once you're logged into your page, you should see something like this ...

To begin the optimization process, make sure you're viewing your Company page in "admin mode." To do this, check the blue bar at the top of the page (as shown above). On the left, you'll see if you're viewing your page as an Admin or Member. On the right, there's a button that lets you toggle between the two options.

Just below the search box in the above image are four sub-navigation options: Updates, Overview, Analytics, Notifications. To optimize your Company page, you'll need to click on Overview, which should display something similar to what you see above.

Let's begin our optimization right at the top of the page. As always, you'll need to follow the image optimization process we laid out in the SEO section of the book to ensure that every one of your LinkedIn Company page images is well optimized.

1. **Cover Image:** This is the long, narrow image at the top of the page. Because of its dimensions, it might be a bit of a challenge to find an image that looks good here. We used a mobile app called Over to create a simple graphic just for our LinkedIn Company page. If you're artistically inclined, this app (or one like it) can do wonders for simple design tasks like this.

   Regardless of where your image comes from, make sure you have permission to use it and that it's in line with your brand's personality. Our cover image is named: "Cuppa-SEO-Web-Design-Madison-WI," which includes SIX relevant keyword phrases, in total.

2. **Logo:** It is positioned to the left of your company name.

3. **Company Name, Industry and Location:** I know it's obvious, but be sure to put in your full company name here. The line that lives below your name (which includes Industry and Location) is typically populated when you set up your page. That said, there's a way to change it here, too, which we'll discuss once we move down the page.

Below these regions are three additional regions: Overview, Jobs, Life.

Overview is where we currently are, and that's all we need to concern ourselves with for optimization purposes.

About
Moving farther down, we find the About section. Similar to your Facebook Business page, it contains multiple regions, starting with your Company Description.

Company Description
Similar to the Story section in Facebook, the Company Description is meant to inform visitors AND LinkedIn about your business, services and/or products.

Since it allows fewer characters than your Facebook Story, your LinkedIn Company Description can be a pared-down version of your Facebook Story, keeping in mind that you are now on a B2B platform.

Cuppa SEO's Company Description is 1,883 characters long.

As you pare down your content, here's another opportunity to freshen it up a bit. If this content replicates your GMB or Facebook Business page, there's a likelihood it will be seen as syndication. Within LinkedIn's algorithm, this may be just fine. But without hard evidence, I never like to take chances — which is why my LinkedIn Company Description is different from what I have on Facebook or GMB.

Here's my complete LinkedIn Company Description ...

Holistic Web Design – SEO – Online Marketing Consulting

HOLISTIC WEB DESIGN
Cuppa SEO creates websites with SEO, user experience and conversion brewed right in.

But what does that mean, in plain English?

Our holistic approach to web design means we build websites that get found, build trust and make it easy for visitors take the next step in becoming a customer. It's an approach that looks at your website as a whole, addressing all of the major success points so it's a fully-functioning site that helps you build your business.

The result is a site with a built-in return on investment (ROI), so you're not just spending money on your website — you're also making money because of it!

The major benefits of holistic web design:
1. Custom Web Design
2. Search Engine Optimization (SEO)
3. User Experience (UX)
4. Conversion
5. Designed for Desktop & Mobile

SEARCH ENGINE OPTIMIZATION (SEO)

SEO increases traffic to your website. When done right, it improves natural ranking in search results, making you easier to find (hence, the increased traffic) — which leads to more sales, better customer engagement and overall growth.

Cuppa SEO can optimize every nook and cranny of your website, including title tags, headlines, images, body copy and text links. We'll also create custom meta descriptions for each of your web pages.

ONLINE MARKETING CONSULTING

Cuppa SEO's Online Marketing Consulting gives you and your your team an in-depth understanding of SEO, user experience and conversion — and shows you how to implement these strategies into your website, blog and social media.

Long-term benefits of our consulting services include:
   - Improved SEO helps increase traffic to your website
   - A better user experience means visitors are more likely to stick around
   - Optimized conversion strategies help visitors take the next step in becoming a customer

Specialties
The next area of the About section is where you can list each of your company's areas of expertise.

Although it's not necessary, I like to list our specialties in alphabetical order for a better user experience. LinkedIn allows you to add up to 20 specialties — yet keep the list as short as possible, as you don't want to be perceived as a jack of all trades (even if you are)! To pare it down to the least number of specialties (if you have a lot of them), consider what makes up 80% of your business and go with those.

The words and phrases you list in your Specialties section help LinkedIn's search engine find you, so it's important to choose the best products- and services-related keywords from your keyword report here (just as we're doing on the rest of the page).

Company Info

Remember a little earlier when we talked about your Company Name, Industry and Location section? This is where you can alter your industry as well as your company's website address, company size, year founded and company type.

Some of these regions offer limited options, and you'll need to choose what's best suited for your company. For instance, there are no "Web Design" or "SEO" choices under LinkedIn's industry selection, so I chose the most accurate option possible: "Marketing and Advertising."

Locations

Next up is your location.

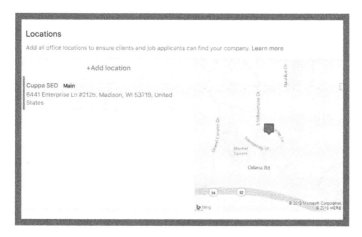

I want to emphasize how important it is to ensure that your address here is EXACTLY as it appears on Facebook, Google My Business, and anywhere else your business is listed. If you're not sure this is the case, you can use a free service like Moz Local (https://moz.com/products/local) to check your major business listings. Google cares, and a consistent address in all your listings can help boost the authority of your site, while inconsistent listings can lower it. It's definitely a form of optimization, and a super-easy one.

Groups

The last piece of the Overview section is your groups. Although there's no way to optimize them, it's a good idea to populate them (accurately) so people know whom you're affiliated with.

If you're in the same group as someone else, it could help facilitate a smoother connection. It also could help qualify your business if someone sees it in a group they respect.

20. UX and Conversion on Your LinkedIn Company Page

Overall, the UX and conversion strategies on your LinkedIn Company page are simpler than your Facebook Business page. There are fewer options to consider and fewer regions to populate. That being said, both are still worth reviewing …

CREATING A SOLID USER EXPERIENCE

The best way to ensure a solid UX on your page is to populate every nook and cranny with accurate, benefit-driven content and imagery.

Take an honest look at your page from the Member View (if you're still in the Manage Page section, just click "Go to member view" to get there).

How does your page look? Are you using original imagery wherever possible? If so, are the images engaging? Do they make people feel at home and comfortable, or does your imagery make you visitors say, "ewww?"

There are only a couple of opportunities to add imagery to your LinkedIn Company page. Make sure they evoke a positive user experience, not an ewww ...

What about the content in your About Us section? Does it highlight the top benefits someone can expect from working with or buying from you? You've heard this before, but it's worth repeating: Clear, customer-centric, benefit-driven content will go a long way in boosting engagement with viewers. Figure out your customer's pain and address it — on your social media channels, your website, in person — everywhere.

If you're not proficient at choosing engaging photos or writing benefit-driven copy, hire someone who is. Even if you are good at these things, it's often helpful to ask a handful of trusted colleagues, customers or friends what they think. A small test group can help clarify whether or not you're providing a positive UX. Don't assume!

Unlike your Facebook Business page, your LinkedIn Company page does not allow you to adjust the hierarchy of information on the page. They want it their way, so just make sure what you implement is the best it can be.

CONVERSION ON YOUR LINKEDIN COMPANY PAGE
LinkedIn, if you're reading this ... we need to talk.

Why oh why don't you have a conversion button available for our LinkedIn Company Pages? Facebook provides one (with a nice amount of customization) ...

It would be super-helpful for any B2B business if there were something similar on our LinkedIn Company Pages. At the time of this writing, alas, there is not.

Our LinkedIn conversion opportunities are pretty limited. The best thing you can do is make sure you've populated the following regions in your Company Details section, so at least a visitor has access to your website:

In addition to a conversion button, it would also be nice if the Company Details section included fields for a business phone number and email address. Honestly, these changes seem like a no-brainer, so let's hope they happen soon!

But there is some good news: As does Facebook, LinkedIn gives you the opportunity to publish posts on your Company Page, and here is where you'll have a better opportunity to implement a solid conversion strategy. I'm getting a little ahead of myself, so let's get started at the beginning of ...

21. SEO, UX and Conversion in Your LinkedIn Company Page Posts

LINKEDIN COMPANY PAGE: PUBLISHING A POST
Publishing on your LinkedIn Company page is similar to publishing a post on your Facebook Business page. And although publishing while sipping a cup of hot coffee is recommended, it is not mandatory.

Let's review the process:

1. Go to your LinkedIn Company Page and click "Manage page" (if you' aren't there already).

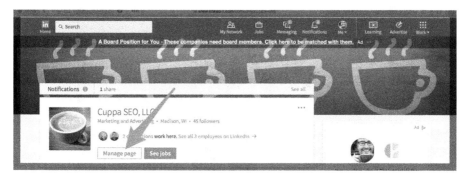

2. Next you'll see a region toward the top that says: "Share an article, photo, video or idea."

3. Click in that region and it will expand (again, just as it does on Facebook), allowing you to add your headline, content, text link (if you're looking to drive visitors to your website or blog), and photo or video.

SEO, UX AND CONVERSION

Here's an example of what a well-constructed LinkedIn Company Page post looks like (It's the same example we used in the Facebook Business Page section) ...

Title (Headline)
What's the Point of Having a Website Nobody Can Find?

The clear, emotionally engaging title is meant to connect with business owners who are frustrated because their website is not getting found — in other words, their sites are not generating enough traffic.

SEO: Whenever possible, I like to include a keyword phrase in the title of my LinkedIn Company Page posts. As you can see, this is NOT the case here. I always like to say, "Never sacrifice the quality of your content for the sake of SEO. Search engine optimization needs to *support* your content, not weaken it."

Here, the emotional engagement I was looking for was paramount, which goes to show there is no one-size-fits-all solution for social media (or anything else, for that matter). Always take a moment to think about what your intention (or goal) is for every single post you publish, and then follow through on that intention.

UX: The title is clear, especially to those who are having problems with website traffic — and those are the folks we want to connect with. The title also offers a good UX to this demographic, because it shows understanding of a serious problem they're experiencing. If people reading the post fit into this category, they might be feeling hurt (even betrayed) by their previous web developer who charged them a premium price for a sub-par website that isn't performing.

The title is further clarified by the brief copy and imagery that follows it.

Conversion: As you might have guessed, conversion doesn't come directly into play in the title. BUT, if the title didn't have a good UX — say it was really long, ambiguous or didn't have an emotional tug — you'd have less chance of someone reviewing the rest of the post and clicking on your link. That's why I consider the title a "soft conversion," or a conversion leader.

Brief Content
Under our headline, the copy reads:

> Cuppa SEO builds sites that get found, build trust & make it easy for visitors to become customers. Sound good? Find out more @ https://lnkd.in/eqrSePy

SEO: Except for "SEO" our copy doesn't have keywords in it. And that's OK, because once again I am trying to engage with readers on an emotional level — and connect with them in terms they understand. So if you're wondering why my example isn't chock-full of keywords, that's why. Your LinkedIn Company Page post content (and title for that matter) may not always be optimized with keywords. If this is the case, it's OK — as long as it's a choice and not an oversight.

I've done a lot of testing and research, and I've found that even my marketing-savvy clients don't respond well to words like "SEO," "user experience" and "conversion." They respond well to knowing that I understand their problem, and that I know how to solve it! Thus, the copy here offers solutions to the problem addressed in the title — in plain English.

UX: As you might have guessed, this content is good for UX because it "pays off" the title and adds clarification. It's also on the short side, which also provides a solid UX. The shorter the better — as long as you're not sacrificing a clear, engaging message for brevity. As we mentioned in the Google My Business section, the content in your post is an appetizer — not a main course. It's meant to entice and engage readers so they are eager to take the next step, which of course is …

Conversion: Once readers have taken the time to read our title and copy, we need to give them a clear, easy path to taking the next step we want them to take. In this case, it's visiting Cuppa SEO's Web Design page. In our example, this is accomplished with a shortened text link (LinkedIn automatically shortens text links in posts; you don't have to worry about it).

Imagery
It's no surprise that imagery is a critical component of your LinkedIn Company Page posts, so let's dive in …

SEO: The image is well optimized. The actual image name is: Cuppa-SEO-Madison-WI-Web-Design-UX-Services.jpg.

As we've discussed before, an optimized image makes your post easier to find on social media and in organic searches. Be sure to optimize your imagery as we outlined earlier in the book.

UX: Your picture/imagery is what I like to call your "stopper," because it can literally stop viewers in their tracks while they're scrolling through their Facebook feed. The picture is your instant UX meter — providing a positive, negative or neutral experience in the blink of an eye. If the image doesn't cause a positive UX, the scrolling continues (which is why choosing or creating engaging imagery is so important).

Your imagery should always support your post's headline and copy. When it does, the overall UX of your post rises. It's all about creating a cohesive post so the reader doesn't have to think about how the copy and the picture go together — because it's obvious.

Conversion: If possible, make sure your imagery is clickable AND that it leads to the content you're highlighting in your post. For example, when clicked, the imagery in our current example leads the reader directly to our Web Design page. But this does not happen by chance, so let's discuss the process ...

To have the imagery in my LinkedIn Company Page post to link directly to my Web Design page, the image first needs to live on my actual Web Design page. In other words, when I created the page, I needed to think ahead and use imagery that would also look good on social media. It needed to be sized correctly (so it fit well in within the parameters of my LinkedIn post), and have a clear message that made sense on my site as well as on social channels.

Once the imagery is on my Web Design page, when I add the link to my Web Design page into my LinkedIn post, LinkedIn automatically pulls the image into the post. Even better, that image is coded (by LinkedIn) to be a direct link to my Web Design page!

Now my image and my text link both drive people to the same place, which is a big plus for conversion (and for UX, too).

On the other hand, if you upload an image directly into your LinkedIn Company Page post (from somewhere like your desktop, Dropbox, or photo library), when clicked it won't lead people to where you want them to go. Instead, it will only make the image bigger — which means you'll potentially lose out on converting someone. Avoid this. Take the time to set things up right, if it's possible to do so.

Holistic Side Note: *The copy you see directly below the image in our example …*

> *"Cuppa SEO creates custom websites with SEO, UX and conversion brewed right in…"*

… is also automatically imported by LinkedIn. If you're wondering where it came from, it's a shortened version of the meta description that was created for the Web Design page (we talked about meta descriptions in the SEO section of the book, too). It's a shortened version because LinkedIn doesn't provide enough characters to display the entire meta description. If you notice that LinkedIn is truncating this content, you can easily edit. All you need to do is click in the region and edit away!

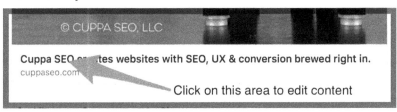

Just be sure to double-check that content looks good before you hit "Post." And be sure to publish your post to the public for greater reach!

A WORD ON LINKEDIN VIDEO

Following on the coattails of Facebook Live, LinkedIn Video provides you with an opportunity to engage with people by recording a live video on LinkedIn or by uploading a pre-recorded video. As of this writing, I have not tested LinkedIn Video, but it is something we will be doing often. With the ever-increasing popularity of video, this is a great way to engage with your LinkedIn audience (as long as your video is engaging and full of helpful content).

SHARING CONTENT ON YOUR LINKEDIN PERSONAL PROFILE

Whether it's a video or a static post, be sure to share everything you publish on your LinkedIn Company page on your LinkedIn Personal Profile.

Why? You want to make sure you gain the most organic reach possible with each post, and often a Personal Profile can have a much wider reach than a Company Profile. For example, Cuppa SEO has only a few dozen followers, although I have over 1,000 connections in my LinkedIn network.

In order to share a Company Page post on your Personal Profile, simply click on the "Share" button at the bottom of the post.

22. LinkedIn Sponsored Updates

Breaking my rule one more time (of not talking about paid forms of online marketing), let's take a brief look at something many people haven't even heard of ... LinkedIn Sponsored Updates.

LinkedIn Sponsored Updates are a way of sharing content you publish on your LinkedIn Company Page with professionals that are NOT in your network. This content can be shared with individuals who work at specific companies, in specific roles (CEO, Marketing Director, etc.), and you can really drill down to a granular level of with whom you'd like to share your content.

Even better (or at least as good) is the fact that a Sponsored Update shows up in the feed of these professionals — just as if they were part of your LinkedIn network.

Here's what one looks like ...

As you can see, the Sponsored Update says "Promoted" in the upper left corner of the post. That's the only difference between a Sponsored Update and a regular LinkedIn post.

You can use Sponsored Updates only on your LinkedIn Company Page, as LinkedIn doesn't allow this service through a Personal Profile.

What better way to connect with the exact people and the exact companies you'd like to do business with? Sponsored Updates are FAR superior to LinkedIn Ads — those little, blurry, odd, often unnoticed things that sometimes sit at the side of your Personal Profile page.

Now that you know about Sponsored Updates, if you're a B2B organization, I highly recommend that you consider testing them.

This brings us to the end of our social media section.

I hope the strategies included here help you improve the SEO, UX and conversion of every single post you publish — and ultimately help your business engage with more people!

THE END

Index

A

A/B testing 216
address
    Google My Business and 278
Adwords 40, 207, 210–211, 281. *See also* Google, Adwords
aesthetic 116, 138, 150, 182
alternate image text (alt text) 87, 89
alt text. *See* alternate image text (alt text)
analog user experience 20, 21, 22, 24, 26, 28, 30, 33, 34
Apple 32, 34, 165

B

backlinks 68, 106, 240
    and ranking 105
    quality of 106
Banana Republic 127, 129, 132
baseball glove analogy 95
black hat SEO 89, 94
"bleets"
    and blogging 231
blog campaign 232
blog content
    fresh 27
blogging 223–245
    and expertise 228
    and relationships 226
    and social media 223
    and the 3C's 226
blog headlines
    and UX 253
blog posts 327
    2–3 sentence overview 233
    excerpts 256–257
    frequency of 5, 15, 225
    full 256
    length of 225
    long-form 231
    scheduling 5, 225

short-form 231
writing 5, 95, 225, 226, 228, 231, 233, 237, 248, 253
blogs 119, 223, 251–259
    and conversion 260–262
    and keywords 227
    and relationships 45, 224, 260
    and SEO 223–224, 236, 238–241, 247–249, 253
    and user experience 230, 251–258
    calls-to-action on 225
    categories 225
    conversion 45, 260–262
    definition of 224
    desktop version 252–254
    fresh content and 15
    hard sell and 45
    headlines 226
    how to write 5, 224, 226–233
    impact on SEO 79
    importance of 4
    increased traffic with 224
    mobile version 256
    optimizing 5, 83, 87, 91, 227, 235, 238, 247–249
    original vs. duplicate content in 5, 225, 239–241
    purpose of 5, 45, 224
    relation to websites 79
    role of social media in 5, 225, 244–245
    sales pitches on 226
    scheduling 232
    subpage versus subdomain for 225
    tags 225
    tags and categories 233
    writing 229
blog sharing 245
blog strategy 47
blog subscriptions 244
blog tags
    and SEO 234

region
  optimizing for 83
regional searching 11
relationship building 48, 260
relationship-building philosophy 76
relationship funnel 61
relationships 21, 32, 45, 53, 272
  and blogging 224
  and networking 272
  social media and 268
relevance testing
  keyword 80
rotating banner 139
rotating offers 139

S

sales funnels
  conversion and 60
  problems with 60
sandwich analogy 98
"sandwich" navigation 117
scrolling website 218
search engine optimization (SEO) 4, 9–17,
        78–112
  and blogs 247–249
  applying 68
  beyond implementation 99–114
  effective 10
  social media and 266
  value 248
search engines 17, 234
  and headlines 227
search results 97
  natural 13, 78
  organic 10
search-to-competition ratio 81
secondary keywords
  number of 95
secondary navigation 117–123
Secure Hypertext Transfer Protocol (HTTPS)
        112
semantic keywords
  number of 95
SEMrush 80
SEO. *See* search engine optimization
SEO implementation 18
SEO pie 10
Short Pixel 110
sidebars
  and mobile sites 258
side navigation 121, 127
single CTA 181
slideshows 139
  and conversion 217
social buttons 124

and navigation 133
social media 3–4, 15, 265–267, 323–324, 333
  and CTAs 211
  and searches 10
  and the Ghostbusters 269–271
  blogging and 15, 48, 223, 265
  campaigns 76, 270–271
  conversion and 48
  importance of 4, 6
  overview of 268
  two sides of 268–269
  websites and 265
social media buttons 136
social media channels 272, 342
social media posts 48, 265
  and conversion 266
  optimizing 15
social proof 136, 158
"soft conversion" 321, 347
"soft sell" CTA 181, 186
squeeze pages 40, 206, 296
  design of 213
sticks 248
stock photos 91, 323
strategies
  UX and conversion 6
"stuffing" 92
subdomains
  and blogs 242
subpages 119, 206, 242
  blogs as 241
  conversion and 69
  design of 156
  user experience and 26, 155
subpage strategy 47
subscribe widget 254
subscription
  blog 254
syndication 304, 336

T

tags
  blog 5
templates
  Facebook Business 314
testing 4, 63, 216, 322, 342, 348
  A/B 216
  importance of accurate data 216
text link
  CTA via 46
text link CTA 46
text links 50, 96, 249, 262, 295, 322
  and keyword phrases 249
  conversion and 49
  crafting 96

ABOUT THE AUTHOR

In addition to running Cuppa SEO, a successful web design firm, Joey offers consulting services and keynote presentations based on the principles found in his book, *A Holistic Guide to Online Marketing.*

Joey's marketing career began over two decades ago as a copywriter working in print and web. Over time, he developed a passion for search engine optimization, which led him to become an expert in the field. The more proficient he became at optimizing websites — and driving more traffic to them — the more he realized the importance of looking at websites, and online marketing, holistically. This sparked intensive study and testing of methodologies including user experience, conversion, and emotional engagement in both the digital and analog world.

Over the years, Joey has had the privilege of working with companies like Promega, Lands' End, The Public Relations Society of America (PRSA), Grainger Industrial Supply, Widen, and many other national and local brands.

Beyond his professional history, who is this guy?

Joey is the dad of two awesome boys, and happily married since 1997. He's a big fan of Zig Ziglar, Dieter Rams, Kenya Hara, mindfulness meditation, essentialism, Field Notes notebooks, family time, skateboarding, geeky tech stuff — and coffee!